Sacred Pathways Journal

THE Desert Walk

A Journey Through Lent with Jesus

Leslie Albizzatti

Liguori Publications
A Redemptorist Ministry
CATHOLIC. PASTORAL. TRUSTED.

I would describe Leslie as a spiritual midwife and prayer warrior. I begin with that because I've experienced firsthand her closeness with the Lord. I trust her prayer and discernment, and, because of that, I trust her as a guide through the desert that is Lent. The meditations in this book echo the timeless spiritual classic He and I in the way Leslie vulnerably shares her conversations and encounters with Jesus. In doing so, she not only allows the reader to witness the beauty of a relationship with God but also invites them to go deeper into their own walk with the Lord.

—Sarah Kroger, Catholic singer/songwriter

The Desert Walk is a beautifully written gem that offers much-needed hydration for the parched, distracted, noise-saturated, and weary soul. Against the backdrop of the desert's stark and sacred landscape, Leslie invites us to journey with her through forty days of honest, intimate, and challenging reflections—drawing us into the heart of Lent and, more deeply, into the heart of Jesus.

This Lenten companion not only offers a rich banquet to feast upon—Sacred Scripture, the wisdom of the saints, and the insights of spiritual masters—but also gently teaches us how to engage the imagination, linger and wrestle in prayer, and vulnerably open our hearts to a fresh and transforming encounter with Jesus. Clearly, Leslie lives and prays under the influence of Jesus. *The Desert Walk* is not just an invaluable companion for Lent, but a soul-nourishing guide for any season.

—Mary Guilfoyle, ACTS XXIX missionary/leadership team

It's physical, this journey through Lent offered by Leslie Albizzatti. Jesus is tangibly with us every step of our journey. We feel his gaze even when we are silent together. We walk a long way, up hills and down again, feeling desert sands and then resting at the base of a cliff. All the while, Jesus coaxes us into the desert, knowing the interior treasures that await us there. Sometimes, he speaks, but usually he quietly awaits our initiative. Jesus lifts our chins, looks into our eyes and hearts, and speaks strong, encouraging words to Lenten pilgrims through this book.

—Fr. Tim Hepburn, pastor, St. Michael Church, Gainesville, Georgia

Any journey with Jesus is worth taking. Leslie gracefully invites each of us to leave behind our comfort and complacency, drawing closer to Jesus and following him on a journey that reveals not only more of him but also more of our own hearts. With humility, gentleness, and honesty, Leslie assures us that we can find him on *The Desert Walk*. The question is, will you come—will you follow where he leads? I'm certain you won't be disappointed if you say "yes."

—Sarah Kaczmarek, director of pastoral ministry, Encounter Ministries

Imprimi Potest:
Kevin Zubel, CSsR, Provincial
Denver Province, The Redemptorists

Published by Liguori Publications
Liguori, Missouri 63057

Liguori Publications, a nonprofit corporation, is an apostolate of the Redemptorists (Redemptorists.com).
To order, visit Liguori.org or call 800-325-9521

ISBN 978-0-7648-2883-6
E-ISBN 978-0-7648-7263-1

Library of Congress Cataloging-in-Publication Data

Names: Albizzatti, Leslie author

Title: The desert walk : a journey through Lent with Jesus / Leslie Albizzatti.

Description: Liguori, MO : Liguori Publications, [2026] | Includes bibliographical references. | Summary: "Daily guided reflections, Scripture readings, and journaling prompts for each day of the Lenten season and Easter Sunday"-- Provided by publisher.

Identifiers: LCCN 2025035270 (print) | LCCN 2025035271 (ebook) | ISBN 9780764828836 paperback | ISBN 9780764872631 ebook

Subjects: LCSH: Catholic Church--Prayers and devotions | Lent--Prayers and devotions

Classification: LCC BX2170.L4 A43 2026 (print) | LCC BX2170.L4 (ebook)
LC record available at https://lccn.loc.gov/2025035270
LC ebook record available at https://lccn.loc.gov/2025035271

Printed in Canada
29 28 27 26 25 / 5 4 3 2 1

Cover illustraton: *Jesus in the Desert*, CraftonArtPrints

To Jesus, because there is no desert walk without him.
And to my family, who believed I could.

"To fall in love with God is the greatest romance;
to seek him, the greatest adventure;
to find him, the greatest human achievement."

SAINT AUGUSTINE OF HIPPO, *CONFESSIONS*

Contents

Preface

In the weeks leading up to Lent, I began asking the Lord what Lent would look like this year: "Lord, how do you want me to walk through this season?" As I prayed, nothing immediately came to the forefront. After repeating this same prayer daily, the answer finally arrived on Ash Wednesday.

My Lenten practices have varied over the years, but one thing they all had in common was privacy. Whether I was giving something up or adding a new spiritual discipline for forty days, my practices were personal, and I held them in secret. No one knew about my Lenten practices except those with whom I chose to share.

In the dawn hour of Ash Wednesday, I began my prayer time with the Lord: "Lord, it's the start of Lent, and I'm not sure what you would like this season to look like. I'm not hearing anything." And then, I heard him speak to my heart.

In my prayerful conversation with the Lord, I sensed his gentle voice saying to me, "Write every morning for the next forty days about our time in the desert and share it."

I replied, "Well, now, let's talk about this, Jesus. I can meet you in the morning, walk with you in the desert, and write about our time together. But share it? I don't think so!" As a social introvert, I like people, but I also like my quiet, hidden interior life, which matches my private nature. I met Jesus' invitation to share my journey with him with some resistance.

"You've got the wrong girl! I can't do this," I flatly told him. We've had these kinds of discussions before, Jesus and me. He asks, and I feel inadequate, full of doubt and uncertainty. Surely, he could find someone more qualified for the task, someone with knowledge and expertise. Yet, he didn't ask someone else. And, although I hemmed and hawed, pushed back, and bargained with Jesus, no matter how daunting and intimidating it felt, I acquiesced to what he had asked of me.

You see, Jesus knows me very well. He knows every one of us very well. If I had known too far ahead of time what the Lord had in store for me, I would have experienced more unnecessary worry, stress, balking, and resisting—of which there certainly was some.

Writing for forty days (excluding Sundays) and sharing it with others on a blog felt like an overwhelming project that would, more importantly, make me too vulnerable for my liking. Figuratively standing, exposed and naked, in front of a crowd is not something I seek, ever. Then again, Jesus never asks anything of us that he hasn't already experienced.

The Desert Walk is based not only on my forty-day Lenten experience—a healing journey that continues today—but also on my prayer life, Scripture meditations, countless journal entries, and years of friendship with Jesus. In writing this book, I hope the daily meditations in the desert will lead you to a more profound friendship with our Lord. May the Holy Spirit guide you and highlight areas for spiritual growth, healing, and transformation. Walking intimately with Jesus and opening our hearts to him changes everything.

I pray that *The Desert Walk* draws you deeper into the heart of our Lord.

"[Jesus] said to them, 'Come, and you will see'" (John 1:39).

Introduction

Why the Desert?

I can never remember if the word "desert" has one "s" or two. Then, I remember that the word with two is much more appealing. The desert doesn't always evoke visions of beauty or excitement, yet there is an allure to this dry, dusty, rocky, and sandy place that has a peculiar beauty of its own. I am often struck by how much life exists in the desert. It appears so desolate at first glance, but a closer look reveals something more. The same is true of our spiritual practice in Lent. What at first seems to be a season for sacrifice and discipline may, in fact, be a time for exposing hidden graces and interior treasures.

While there are undoubtedly many picturesque locations that can help foster a deep connection with the Lord and prepare us for Easter, the desert, with its stark beauty and hidden life, invites us to explore and discover new depths of our faith, offering us a unique experience unlike any other time of the year. Stepping into the desert's silence during Lent can be a much-needed respite from the clamor and chaos of the world. We all yearn for peace and silence, whether we're aware of it or not. The quiet moments spent with the Lord can bring healing and restoration, soothing our concerns, discontent, and pain.

Our Lord's Voice in the Stillness

As I contemplate the desert for Lent, three characteristics come to mind: the scenery, the silence, and the shelter.

First, the barren scenery of the desert makes it a place of austerity. It offers few disturbances, which is a tremendous blessing during Lent. Focusing on the Lord is easier when we don't allow ourselves to be consumed by diversion and distraction.

Second, the desert is a place of profound silence. In this silence, God's voice becomes clearer. The world's constant buzz can often drown out his whispers, making it difficult to hear him. But in the solitude of the desert, in the quiet of our hearts, we can more readily hear his voice. As the Lord beckons us into the desert, into the stillness, he invites us to listen to his voice above all others.

Third, as a nature lover, I think about the extreme climate in the desert, where Jesus spent forty days and nights exposed to severe conditions. Where does one find refuge from the harsh elements? Shelter is sparse in this type of terrain. There are no shade trees and few natural hiding places. A journey into the desert leaves us vulnerable and asks that our authentic selves step forward. We will need to find shelter not in a place, but in the person of Jesus Christ.

The Format

There are forty reflections in this book: one for each day of Lent, from Ash Wednesday to Holy Saturday, and a final reflection on Easter Sunday. Each day begins with a quote, followed by the daily theme, a Scripture verse for meditation, and a few questions for journaling. The time for each reflection may average between 15 and 30 minutes, or more if desired. Sundays are for rest on the Lord's Day; the Sunday gospel verses provided are for pondering the goodness of the Lord.

This is your time with Jesus. If he takes you in a completely different direction instead of the theme for the day, follow it. He will reveal exactly what you need for that day. *The Desert Walk* is merely a guide to help you connect with your heart and his.

The Desert Walk is a sacred pathway that takes you through a prayer experience with Jesus, a progression to move from an outer spiritual life of doing and performing to an interior life of abiding and being in communion with the Lord. Simply put, it is moving from busyness to stillness and from the head to the heart.

Contemplative prayer and imaginative prayer are powerful tools to encounter the living Christ; they foster a deeper interior life. This journey of prayer begins with quiet time for listening, getting in touch with the senses, and experiencing the Lord's presence. With time, this type of prayer can yield beautiful fruit.

Journaling can also be a key component of prayer. Writing thoughts, feelings, prayers, inspirations, and sensory impressions help us internalize what we are experiencing through the visual practice of seeing those thoughts and feelings in writing. Journaling can be sentences or pages long, or it can be simply a list of words and bullet points. It can be sketches or abstract drawings. The idea is to put pen to paper and let the Holy Spirit work through your body, mind, and spirit.

Lent is a precious gift: a time to pray, reflect, look inward, and draw closer to Christ. It is a special season in the life of the Church dedicated to preparing ourselves spiritually for Easter. This journey encourages us to focus and walk intentionally with Jesus through the Lenten desert, sharing in his passion and cross, and ultimately celebrating his glorious resurrection on Easter Sunday.

Join me in accepting this invitation into the Lenten desert—a silent, peaceful place with few distractions, where you can be in the company of Jesus to hear his voice and connect deeply with his heart. Although the desert may initially appear as a lonely, arid landscape, it gradually reveals its abundant beauty as we follow Jesus and cultivate a profound friendship with him.

"I will lead her into the wilderness and speak persuasively to her" (Hosea 2:16b).

About Spiritual Journaling

1. What Is Spiritual Journaling?

At its heart, spiritual journaling is the practice of writing to deepen your relationship with God. It's not merely about putting words on a page, but engaging your mind, heart, and soul in response to God's presence and revelation in your life. Through reflection, prayerful writing, and honesty, you create space for God to speak and for you to listen, remember, and respond.

For centuries, spiritual seekers—from biblical figures to modern-day saints—have written down their prayers, struggles, questions, insights, and hopes. This practice helps us integrate what we hear, learn, and experience into our faith journey.

Think of your journal as a sacred space on paper—one that no one else needs to see but God and you. It is a place where you can be real, vulnerable, and authentic. As you write, your pen becomes a tool of prayer, and your journal becomes a record of grace. Spiritual journaling allows you to reflect on your personal experience as you begin to articulate what faith means for you. The intention is not academic mastery, but transformation. By writing regularly, you allow the Holy Spirit to work deeply and personally in you.

2. Who Is This Book For?

Whether you are brand-new to the faith or longing to grow in your spiritual life, this book, with its thought-provoking journal prompts, welcomes you as you are. You don't need to be a skilled writer or a theologian. All you need is to be open to letting God meet you on these pages.

3. Theological Foundations for Journaling

Faith Seeking Understanding (St. Anselm)

The Catholic faith is not just received—it is lived in. Saint Anselm described theology as "faith seeking understanding." Journaling is one way to seek understanding—not only intellectually but also emotionally and spiritually.

The Example of the Saints
Many saints practiced spiritual journaling. Consider:

- Saint Augustine, whose *Confessions* remains one of the most profound journals of the soul ever written.
- Saint Thérèse of Lisieux, who wrote her *Story of a Soul* as a spiritual memoir filled with simple honesty and deep insight.
- Saint Alphonsus Liguori, who taught that spiritual exercises—including writing—help root us in God's will and love.

Writing is a way of praying, thinking, and listening all at once.

4. How to Use This *Sacred Pathways* Book

Think of this book as a companion on *your* sacred pathway. You are free to write as much or as little as you like. What matters is that you return to it regularly.

You'll find:

- Journaling prompts throughout this book.
- Scripture references and prayers to inspire reflection.
- Space to write freely, doodle, paste, or draw if you'd like.

Establish a rhythm:

- Read the prompt.
- Reflect quietly.
- Write from the heart. Don't worry about grammar or form.
- Revisit your writing later for further insight.

5. Tips for Journaling Spiritually

1. Begin with prayer. Ask the Holy Spirit to guide your thoughts.
2. Be honest. This is your space. You can wrestle with questions, express doubts, and record joys.
3. Use Scripture. Let a Bible verse spark your thoughts. Many of the reflections and prompts include Scripture references.
4. Be consistent. A few lines in response to each prompt build a powerful record of your faith.
5. Review often. Flip back through previous pages. Notice how your understanding and relationship with God is growing.

6. Journaling as Transformation

Writing is not simply remembering—it is forming. It integrates:

- The mind (understanding and concepts).
- The heart (prayer and feeling).
- The will (commitment and action.)

Through journaling, faith becomes more than ideas—it becomes a lived experience. Your journal will become:

- A mirror for self-discovery.
- A repository of insights and prayers.
- A map of your spiritual journey.

In moments of dryness or doubt, you can look back and remember how God has led you thus far.

7. A Word from the Tradition

> *"The one who desires to be saved must continually examine the state of his soul, and journaling is a most useful exercise for such reflection." —St. Alphonsus Liguori*

The Church invites us to not just learn the faith but to live and embody it. Writing brings this invitation to life. It enables you to pause amid the rush of new information and hear what God is saying personally to you.

8. Your Journey Starts Here

Let this journaling be a space of:

- Stillness in a noisy world.
- Clarity in a confusing time.
- Faith in the midst of questions.
- Each page is a step in your walk with God.

Welcome to the journey. Welcome home.

Rev. Thomas M. Santa, CSsR
Liguori Publications

Tips to Handle Distractions

1. Keep a notebook handy or use the space provided in this book to record distractions.
2. Turn the distraction into a prayer for the person or situation that occupies your thoughts.
3. Pray 2 Corinthians 10:5: "take every thought captive in obedience to Christ."
4. Meditate on a word or phrase—such as Jesus, Yeshua, Beloved—and keep repeating it.
   Or, create your own words or phrases that help you focus on the Lord.
5. Practice breathing exercises.
6. Listen to worship music.

Day 1

The Invitation

(ASH WEDNESDAY)

"I have always loved the desert. One sits down on a desert sand dune, sees nothing, hears nothing. Yet through the silence something throbs, and gleams."

ANTOINE DE SAINT-EXUPÉRY, *THE LITTLE PRINCE*

Standing at the edge of the Lenten desert, I am captivated by the immense and daunting landscape that unfolds before me. As far as the eye can see, there are infinite particles of sand and rock stretching endlessly into the horizon.

My wandering thoughts keep me company as I stare intensely at the sand near my feet. There is no obligation for me to step into the desert. I can choose whether to embark on this Lenten journey or not. Yet, something or someone is drawing me in. I turn around and observe the lush and tempting comforts of my complacency.

Struggling with the allure to avoid the desert journey, tension builds within me. Thoughts of worldly indulgence and self-gratification bring a fleeting sense of delight. I like the things of this good world. It is hard to leave them behind. Perhaps, I like them too much.

As the distractions fade, I'm aware of the invitation from Jesus to draw closer to him. But distractions still persist, and the present moment gives way to questions about how this journey will unfold. Will it be arduous or uncomfortable? What if nothing happens? Or what if things surface in my heart that I would rather avoid? Does everyone feel this way at the start of Lent?

The invitation awaits—a chance to journey purposefully with Jesus. Familiarity with the annual Lenten season brings forth the same apprehensions and doubts, fueled by fears of disappointment in myself and unfulfilled commitments.

Why Lent? Its purpose is clear: it is a spiritual preparation for Easter. Yet, I grapple with the discipline and sacrifices it demands. I focus more on what I might give up rather than what I could gain from this journey with the Lord. What is this telling me about myself?

The love-hate relationship with Lent is laced with uneasiness and expectation. Dread lingers, for the desert seems unwelcoming. Yet, my anticipation arises: *What will my time with Jesus bring? Do I really want to expose myself to this? What if it doesn't unfold as expected?* And so, I offer myself silent reassurance: *The only way forward is to take the plunge.*

I close my eyes, take a deep breath, and utter a prayer: "Jesus, guide me through this desert journey and open my heart to all you have in store for me." Hesitation marks my first step, but I reach for his hand and leave behind the familiar comforts. I step into the unknown, trusting in the guiding presence of the Holy Spirit. We stand together in the sand. It is warm, gritty, and coarse beneath my feet.

Scripture

"[The Lord said,] 'They shall not hunger or thirst; nor shall scorching wind or sun strike them; For he who pities them leads them and guides them beside springs of water.'"

Isaiah 49:10

Reflection

1. As you take that first step into the desert, pause and tune in to your surroundings. What are you feeling? What do you sense or see around you? Let your thoughts flow freely.
2. As you consider accepting Jesus' invitation, what hopes surface within you? Are there any hesitations or doubts that linger? Take a moment to journal your experience—be honest with yourself.
3. Visualize the encounter. Close your eyes and imagine yourself standing in the desert with Jesus by your side. What does he want to reveal to you at this moment? Allow his presence to speak to your heart.

Day 2

First Step

"Lent is a time of returning to God. It is a time to confess how we keep looking for joy, peace, and satisfaction in 'many lovers' without being faithful to our first love."

HENRI NOUWEN, *SABBATICAL JOURNEY: THE DIARY OF HIS FINAL YEAR*

Standing in the sand, I look back at the abundance of the world, which will soon grow faint in the distance. Pensive and quiet, I hold Jesus' calloused hand. I have known Jesus for a while, and, like in all relationships, my trust and love have grown as the years have passed. Jesus is gentle and patient, never harsh. At the heart of any relationship is love—an act born of free will, not coercion, persuasion, or force. Jesus waits for me to take another step.

The tempter urges me to leave the desert and abandon this Lenten journey. The glitter and glamour of worldly enticements make false promises of fulfillment. The tempter mocks, "It's not too late! It would be easy to turn back, and who would ever know?"

The "what ifs" feel more numerous than the countless grains of sand. When they arise, I am plagued with doubts and lack of self-confidence. Questioning my ability, I stop moving forward. "What ifs" are stumbling blocks to taking a step, while each step forward is progress in trusting in the Lord.

I refocus and remind myself that staying committed to the desert experience is the right thing to do. Consequently, I dismiss the temptations. Jesus waits as my mind races with questions, insecurities, and fears. He whispers, "Put them aside." The soothing sound of his voice stills my rambling mind. It is a voice I recognize, and his words bring calm. I am reminded that Peace stands close to me. Jesus asks me to put aside the fears, doubts, and worries and to follow him. The insecurities will surface from time to time; however, it's important to remember that trust in Jesus overcomes everything else.

A line in the sand seems to separate everything in the world from everything in the desert. Taking a deep breath, I notice the smells of the desert: the air is dry and the fragrances unfamiliar. Each step is a choice to move ahead instead of remaining spiritually stagnant. Why do I hesitate to move forward? Tightening my grip on Jesus' hand, the world's hold begins to loosen. I take another step. The distractions and allure of the world start to fade into the distance.

Scripture

"[Jesus said,] 'Peace I leave with you; my peace I give to you. Not as the world gives do I give it to you. Do not let your hearts be troubled or afraid.'"

JOHN 14:27

Reflection

1. Journal any questions, insecurities, or fears that surface as you contemplate taking your first steps into the desert. Is there anything holding you back?
2. What words of encouragement do you need from Jesus to keep moving forward? Reflect on his guidance and consider what you might need to release or put aside as you enter this desert experience.
3. Close your eyes and picture yourself vividly with Jesus by your side in the desert. What does the desert look like? What do you notice? What words of his come to mind? Note any thoughts or insights that emerge in the Lord's presence.

Day 3

Detachment

"As long as anything holds me back, I cannot freely fly to you. A simple and pure intention sees God and aims at him alone."

THOMAS À KEMPIS, *THE IMITATION OF CHRIST*

I still feel the persistent pull of the modern world. It possesses the things we prefer not to go without; the things we reach for that bring us comfort—tea steeped to perfection, a warm bed, a hot shower, and countless other conveniences. I contemplate being *in* the world, but not *of* the world. Looking back, I see the indented footsteps in the sand marking the trail thus far.

The world's allure is powerful, like metal drawing a magnet. It is a struggle to detach from worldly things. Wanting to be released from the world and yet longing for it simultaneously, I ask myself what keeps me captive. I reposition my hand and tighten my grip on Jesus' hand.

Jesus begins to lead me, and I follow behind. Walking beside him would be my preference; however, I glance back again at the world I'm leaving behind like a child reluctant to leave a toy store. The world tugs at my heart. It has the things we like, offering the comforts we know and enjoy. Perhaps we enjoy it all too much. I am reminded that worldly pleasures are temporal, and I begin to contemplate temperance.

Jesus says, "Come, child." His words, though few, pierce my heart. One cannot gaze simultaneously in two directions. What does my heart honestly yearn for? Shifting my gaze from the world toward Jesus, my internal dialogue quiets. What he offers is far greater than anything the world can give.

Stepping farther into the desert, I notice that the monotonous landscape presents stillness and silence, yet it feels awkward and uncomfortable. I look around. Actually, my eyes *dart* around; that is a more appropriate way to describe my surveying—perhaps it is a habit formed by constant distraction or fear of missing out.

Jesus looks at me and smiles. It is a smile that makes me feel understood—idiosyncrasies and all. Jesus reminds me of a recent time in prayer when he brought the word "focus" to my mind. It seems appropriate at this moment too. I return his smile but feel a bit uneasy; my mind is buzzing with details and practicalities. Do we have supplies for this journey? What about food, water, and shelter? The questions spin uselessly. What is this need in me to be so prepared? Doesn't everyone have this same need?

Focusing on Jesus and detaching from worldly comforts seems a wiser approach than being preoccupied by a never-ending list of preparatory measures. Detaching from the things I cannot control—situations, relationships, and outcomes—will take practice.

I transition from walking behind Jesus to walking beside him. Gazing at Jesus restores my interior stillness and peace.

Scripture

"Then [Jesus] said to all, 'If anyone wishes to come after me, he must deny himself and take up his cross daily and follow me.'"

LUKE 9:23

Reflection

1. Pope Francis wrote, "Today we can recognize that we fed ourselves on dreams of splendor and grandeur, and ended up consuming distraction, insularity, and solitude. We gorged ourselves on networking, and lost the taste of fraternity. We looked for quick and safe results, only to find ourselves overwhelmed by impatience and anxiety" (*Fratelli Tutti*, 33). What distractions or creature comforts are pulling your attention away from Jesus? Take a moment to journal about this, being honest about what might be diverting your focus.
2. Consider the impact of detachment. If there are things, people, or circumstances you feel called to detach from, reflect on the potential benefits or outcomes. How might letting go positively influence your spiritual journey and personal growth?
3. Close your eyes and imagine yourself in the presence of Jesus. What insights or feelings arise as you contemplate letting go and drawing closer to him?

Day 4

Release

"Come, true light. Come, eternal light. Come, hidden mystery.
Come, nameless treasure. Come, ineffable delight.
Come, light that never sets...
Come, O Holy Spirit, and make your dwelling in us."

SAINT SYMEON THE NEW THEOLOGIAN, *THE HYMNS OF DIVINE LOVE*, HYMN 15

The sight of the barren desert speaks of emptiness. Surveying the landscape, I find it hard to embrace the dry, dusty conditions and let go of the excesses the world offers. As I acclimate to these surroundings, my concerns about preparedness linger. My mind starts churning out questions: *What if I don't do it? What if there's a need I can't fulfill? What if I have to rely on someone else or ask for help? What if it doesn't turn out the way I want?* I am at a loss for answers; it will take time to unearth.

Jesus and I sit quietly to pray and ponder. The beauty of silence is that it allows words to bubble to the surface. Silence creates space for interior movements. Words begin to emerge—"self-reliance," "self-sufficiency," "self-dependence," "self-support." I am taken aback and blush at the presence of so much "self." I'm not leaving much room for the Holy Spirit to move amidst all my focus on self. I pray, "Lord, how do I find balance? How can I do my part and not interfere with the movement of the Holy Spirit? How can I cooperate with You?"

Jesus gently asks, "What is your motivation?" My motivation for being prepared? That's a tough question. I look down for a moment, studying the grains of sand and rocks, and consider what is driving my need to be prepared. I suppose I want to appear as if I have it all together—that I am dependable in getting the job done.

Jesus and I walk together, but his question preoccupies me. I connect with the words that are running through my consciousness—self-reliance, self-sufficiency, self-dependence, self-support. Jesus highlights for me that trying to be in control is a barrier to the Holy Spirit's movement. He reminds me that the Holy Spirit is my guide and advocate, and that following the Spirit requires release. Being led by the Spirit means letting go of control over situations, people, and outcomes. Cooperation with the Holy Spirit yields the fruit of peace. That is how I will know that release has occurred.

My heart yearns for the Holy Spirit to move and direct me more freely. I close my eyes and pray, "Jesus, I am sorry for the barriers I have built to block the movement of the Spirit and for the control I am trying to exercise. Lord, teach me to release the areas where I am trying to affect outcomes, preventing the Holy Spirit from taking the lead."

The battle for control is a frequent affliction. Certain that I will need much practice when it comes to releasing, I again pray, "Lord, help me release what I grip tightly. May I place all my trust in you."

Scripture

"Trust in the LORD with all your heart, on your own intelligence do not rely; In all your ways be mindful of him, and he will make straight your paths."

PROVERBS 3:5–6

Reflection

1. Is the Lord asking you to release something into his hands? What fears arise when you think about surrendering control? Reflect on what is holding you back.
2. Are there any spiritual barriers in your life that hinder the movement of the Holy Spirit? Take a moment to identify, acknowledge, and reflect on these obstacles in your journal.
3. Close your eyes and envision yourself with Jesus. As you surrender control to him, what do you experience? Record your thoughts and feelings as you release your fears into his care.

First Sunday of Lent

Gospel Verse

"[Jesus said,] 'One does not live by bread alone,
but by every word that comes forth from the mouth of God.'"

MATTHEW 4:4

Day 5

Abide

"Jesus invites us to abide in his love. That means to dwell with all that I am in him. It is an invitation to a total belonging, to full intimacy, to an unlimited being-with. The light of the Spirit reveals to us that love conquers all fear."

HENRI NOUWEN

"Child, why is your mind so rushed?" Jesus asks. But, I don't know. It seems I woke up this way. My mind easily jumps from thought to thought and bounces from place to place on days when I think I have too much to do to spend time being still.

As Jesus and I walk, I hear the sound of the sand compressing beneath our feet. The rhythmic pattern of our walking begins to soothe my mind. In the distance is a large cluster of rocks, and we make our way toward them. Upon arrival, we sit down to rest. Sitting with Jesus seems to quiet my spirit as his powerful presence of peace washes over me.

It is hard to focus. I drift in and out of being present to Jesus, yet he remains constant and patient. Realizing the need to quiet the mind and be still, I pray, "Lord, calm my racing thoughts and take hold of these distractions. Help me to dwell with you."

The serene and quiet desert helps me start the process of releasing my thoughts and distractions to Jesus. When what whirls within seems inextinguishable, the process of letting go must be intentional. Turning from the desert's vastness to face Jesus directly changes my perspective from feeling overwhelmed to being more peaceful. A Scripture passage from John 15 about remaining—or abiding—in love comes to mind. I want to abide with Jesus, stay focused on him, rest in him, and live in his love and peace. (See John 15:1–10.) But abiding is hard. Staying busy seems easier; perhaps "doing things" has become an ingrained habit. However, the desire to abide and rest with Jesus must outweigh everything else.

Wrestling with what it means to abide, I remember Lazarus' sisters, Martha and Mary. One was busy, rushing and doing; the other was abiding and resting with Jesus. The tension between *doing* and *being* seems irreconcilable, but Jesus perfectly embodies the two.

Focusing on Jesus' presence, I look at him and give him my full attention, which is truly all I have to offer. This offering consists of releasing and letting go of what I cannot control; it is trusting in his ways and in his timing, not in mine. Abiding means surrendering to dwell fully with Jesus. By giving him everything—body, mind, and spirit—we receive his peace.

Handing over all struggles, concerns, distractions, joys, celebrations, and triumphs allows us to experience the fullness of abiding. Abiding in his love brings the peace that I long for: "the peace of God that surpasses all understanding" (Philippians 4:7).

As I consider what it means to truly abide in God, I think, *Although worldly matters vie for our attention, time, and presence, if we better understood the heart of the Father, would wandering from him even be an option?*

Scripture

"Remain in me, as I remain in you. Just as a branch cannot bear fruit on its own unless it remains on the vine, so neither can you unless you remain in me. I am the vine, you are the branches. Whoever remains in me and I in him will bear much fruit, because without me you can do nothing. Anyone who does not remain in me will be thrown out like a branch and wither; people will gather them and throw them into a fire and they will be burned. If you remain in me and my words remain in you, ask for whatever you want and it will be done for you. By this is my Father glorified, that you bear much fruit and become my disciples. As the Father loves me, so I also love you. Remain in my love."

John 15:4–9

Reflection

1. Read Luke 10:38–42. Are you more like Martha or Mary? In what way? Reflect on how their stories resonate with your current journey.
2. Where is the Lord inviting you to a deeper surrender and trust? Imagine offering Jesus the people or situations that hinder your ability to truly abide with him. Take time to journal these offerings.
3. Visualize abiding with Jesus. Close your eyes and sit with Jesus on a large rock in the desert. As you abide in his presence, feel his love surrounding you. What do you sense or receive in this moment?

Day 6

Self

"Jesus points out to me the only way which leads to Love's furnace—that way is self-surrender—it is the confidence of the little child who sleeps without fear in its father's arms."

SAINT THÉRÈSE OF LISIEUX, *STORY OF A SOUL: THE AUTOBIOGRAPHY OF ST. THÉRÈSE OF LISIEUX*

As the days go by, life in the desert becomes increasingly manageable. The once-barren scenery now holds a unique allure. Its tranquil pace starkly contrasts with the hurried and pressured rhythm of the outside world, allowing for easier, perhaps even deeper, breathing.

The dry air carries a distinct scent—an earthy and herbal fragrance mingled with dust and sand. The silence offers comfort and peace, a balm for my often restless spirit. The stillness and quiet nurture the interior life, providing a soothing effect on my soul. Tranquility and solace find a more prominent place when resting with Jesus. Preoccupations seem to fade away.

The concept of "self" comes to mind. I try to identify where my ways might be interfering with God's ways. I recall the words of the LORD: "For my thoughts are not your thoughts, nor are your ways my ways.... For as the heavens are higher than the earth, so are my ways higher than your ways, my thoughts higher than your thoughts" (Isaiah 55:8–9).

As we sit quietly, Jesus calls to mind my service to others. He expresses the goodness in dedicating time and committing energy to those in need. Reflecting on my involvement in a service organization, I realize that my desire to make the organization "successful" has caused me to lose focus on God's ways. In my effort to manage it according to what "self" desires, I have mistakenly assumed ownership of something that isn't mine. Authentic stewardship and service that fall in line with the will of God brings peace. However, in my attempts to serve, sometimes I forget that I don't own the work, the project, the child I'm raising, the people I'm trying to assist. They're not all about "self"; rather, they're fundamentally for God's greater glory.

Gazing into the distance, I understand that claiming ownership leads to self-focused ideas and directives. Where else have I tried to claim ownership and control of situations or people? Through prayer, humility, and surrender, "self" is subdued, making space for the Holy Spirit to move freely, but it's still hard to surrender control.

Further introspection reveals that claiming ownership leads to pride, and pride impedes the Holy Spirit's work. I pray, "Lord, I apologize for holding onto things too tightly and trying to control them—even when it's my involvement in service in your name! Help me to open my hands and to surrender, release, and offer my ministerial service back to you; it was always yours."

The Lord reminds me that we are caretakers, not owners. Embracing humility and meekness rather than pride and stubbornness is key. Keeping "self" in check is difficult. He encourages me to spend more time with him, discussing the work he has called me to do. Though convicted by pride, surrender and honesty bring relief and peace.

Scripture

"Jesus answered and said to them, 'Amen, amen, I say to you, a son cannot do anything on his own, but only what he sees his father doing; for what he does, his son will do also.'"

John 5:19

Reflection

1. Is the Lord urging you to surrender something or someone in your life? Are there situations in which you feel the temptation to take back control? Pause and journal your thoughts, acknowledging any struggles or fears.
2. When you're tempted to reclaim control, how might it feel in that moment to invite the Holy Spirit's guidance instead? Reflect on the peace and trust that could come from letting go, and jot down your feelings.
3. Close your eyes and imagine yourself in the presence of Jesus. What do you experience in this sacred moment? Write about your encounter, capturing the emotions and insights that arise.

Day 7

Vulnerability

"Friendship and love are impossible without a mutual vulnerability."

HENRI NOUWEN, *OUT OF SOLITUDE: THREE MEDITATIONS ON THE CHRISTIAN LIFE*

The desert's tranquil embrace settles deeper within me, and I welcome its calming effects. Perhaps you, too, are beginning to feel the desert's quiet influence. I offer heartfelt gratitude to Jesus for his constant presence; his companionship is my unwavering comfort. Amid life's bustling tempo, I realize how often busyness keeps me from noticing his presence. I look at Jesus with contrition, and he meets me with a gentle, warm smile—a tangible expression of his love.

Love is a funny thing. It is an elusive and multifaceted emotion that is not always easy to define. It is an experience, an inner feeling of assurance that varies from person to person. Ask anyone about love, and you're likely to get as many different responses as the people you ask. For some people, it is too difficult to explain. We each experience love uniquely.

Jesus suggests that we get up off the rock where we've been sitting together and go for a walk. We venture farther into the desert. Here, amidst the stillness, opportunities for reflection, prayer, and introspection abound. In this vast solitude, distractions fade away, leaving space for deeper contemplation.

Lately, the word "cherish" has been percolating in my thoughts. To cherish is to safeguard, to tenderly care for another, to hold close in one's heart and mind. To be loved and cherished is the desire of my heart; it is every person's deepest desire.

My spirit stirs, and Jesus says, "Love requires vulnerability. To be vulnerable requires action." I lose myself in his words and ponder the demands of authentic love with a willingness to let down the barriers guarding my heart. True intimacy requires a courageous act of vulnerability. I whisper to Jesus, acknowledging that I must let down my guard and identify and remove the barriers I've built over time around my heart.

Contemplating Adam and Eve in the Garden of Eden, I envision their profound connection with God, their Creator and Father. Before sin entered the world, they stood fully vulnerable before him, freely sharing their souls and experiencing the fullness of his love. But with sin came guilt and shame, prompting them to hide themselves from their Father. Perhaps hiding is in some way inherited from our first parents and now encouraged by a world that tells us vulnerability equates to weakness.

Do I live as if I truly believe that God's love is indeed infinite, unwavering, and unconditional? I pose this question not to doubt God's love, but to challenge myself to look inward and examine the hidden recesses of my heart. Am I willing to bare my soul, to be vulnerable before God and the loved ones I hold dear?

In the unforgiving desert landscape, where heat scorches the sand during the day, and temperatures drop to near freezing at night, finding shelter is crucial for survival. Jesus points out the natural hideaways: the holes and burrows in the desert floor that provide refuge for the animals. This serves as a powerful metaphor for the refuge we seek from the harsh elements of the world. Amid our own insecurities, fears, and brokenness, we hide. Yet, even in our most hidden places, Jesus, the Good Shepherd, seeks us out, asks us to come out of hiding, and encourages us to embrace greater vulnerability so we can fully receive all he offers.

Scripture

"When they heard the sound of the LORD God walking about in the garden at the breezy time of the day, the man and his wife hid themselves from the LORD God among the trees of the garden. The LORD God then called to the man and asked him: 'Where are you?'"

GENESIS 3:8–9

Reflection

1. Reflect on being loved. How do you desire to be loved and cherished? Recall and record an experience where you truly felt loved or cherished, noting the emotions it evoked.
2. How does Jesus' call to embrace vulnerability challenge you to step out of your comfort zone? How does this invitation push you to grow and change?
3. Explore hidden places. Listen to the song "Out of Hiding (Father's Song)" by Steffany Gretzinger. She sings, "Come out of hiding / You're safe here with me / There's no need to cover what I already see." Journal your thoughts as you listen to the lyrics.
4. Close your eyes and imagine peering into the depths of a burrow with Jesus, representing the hidden places in your heart. Listen closely to what he wants to say to you in this sacred space and record your impressions.

Day 8

Lean In

"Relying on God has to begin all over again every day as if nothing had yet been done."

C.S. LEWIS, *LETTERS TO MALCOLM: CHIEFLY ON PRAYER*

After the first week in the desert, my initial hesitations about this journey have faded, and I look forward to more time with Jesus, curious about what my moments with him will bring.

There is something about walking that feels therapeutic. The repetitive motion of each step requires no thought, and the sparse desert environment offers few distractions, easing my mind and spirit. Our pace is casual, and time with Jesus has opened my heart.

I begin to share: "Lord, trailblazing is lonely." He acknowledges my revelation with a nod. Walking through life without directional signs or landmarks feels like trailblazing. Creating paths and figuring out the best routes can be exhausting and discouraging. My faith journey seems similar, lacking a roadmap and often filled with challenges. Realizing I'm speaking to the true Trailblazer, in every sense of the word, I smile.

"Who are your companions?" Jesus asks. I can think of a few. "Lean in," he says. This is an often-used phrase, but what does it really mean to lean into someone? I recall lyrics from the Bill Withers song "Lean On Me": "Lean on me, when you're not strong / And I'll be your friend / I'll help you carry on." How can anyone help me if I don't express a need?

The song continues to play in my mind: "Please swallow your pride / If I have things you need to borrow / For no one can fill / Those of your needs / That you won't let show." The truth of these lyrics resonates deeply. I pause at the realization that I am slow to ask for help. Pride often stops people, including me, from opening our hearts and sharing with our companions. Embracing vulnerability will require intentionality.

I delve deeper. Where do I need to swallow my pride? Why is it so hard to ask for help? The quiet time in the desert helps me look inward to unearth these answers. My fear of judgment and need to display strength to mask insecurities percolate to the surface. The truth is, God provides the precious gift of his companionship and the gift of friends to help carry the load. It's a matter of asking for help and practicing "leaning in"—being vulnerable and honest with God and our loved ones.

I stop to look back at the distance we've covered. Though many miles remain ahead, a cadence in our steps has evolved. Walking with a friend is comforting.

Scripture

"Humble yourselves before the Lord and he will exalt you."
JAMES 4:10

Reflection

1. Think about moments in your life when you needed help. Were you able to lean on your companions for support? If not, what held you back? Take some time to explore these feelings.
2. Consider a current situation in which you could take the risk of being vulnerable and leaning into a friendship. How might this openness change your experience and strengthen your connection with your friend?
3. Envision Jesus' presence. Close your eyes and imagine yourself with Jesus. What do you feel in his presence? Allow this moment to guide your thoughts and emotions.

Day 9

Love

"[God,] you are good and all-powerful, caring for each one of us as though each is the only one in your care."

SAINT AUGUSTINE OF HIPPO, *CONFESSIONS*

Love. It's a four-letter word that seems simple, yet it carries a depth beyond our earthly understanding. For some, love is commonplace; for others, it remains an enigma. We use the word to describe our feelings about everything from food, clothing, and movies to people. But I am contemplating a different kind of love—a sacrificial love that is ever-present and never ceases to give. The presence of love, the receptivity to love, the experience of love, and the acceptance of love fill my mind. What is true love?

In the distance, a tall ridge beckons, and Jesus guides us toward it. The flat terrain slowly transitions into a challenging ascent, with sand and rocks shifting beneath our feet. Upon reaching the top, I see a vast expanse of sand and rock stretching to the horizon. My initial observation is that it isn't particularly interesting or intriguing, but the immensity of it emerges.

Fatigue sets in after the arduous climb. Looking at Jesus, I wonder why he has brought us here. I say to him, "Jesus, my mind is sluggish today, and I can't seem to connect the dots." He sits down and begins to draw in the sand. I sigh and sit down with him.

The word "extravagant" surfaces as I gaze out over the large canvas of desert sand. The lyrics of a song titled "Extravagant" by Bethel Music echo in my mind: "It's extravagant / It doesn't make sense / We'll never comprehend / The way you love us / It's unthinkable / Only heaven knows / Just how far you'd go / To say you love us." I want to understand extravagant love, but my mind struggles to comprehend it. Intellectualizing love can turn it into a tangled concept; love is meant for the heart. The desert's vastness mirrors the consistency, expansiveness, and endlessness of the Lord's love. He gently turns my head to face him and says, "Take it in."

I reflect on the words "presence," "receptivity," "experience," and "acceptance"—the thoughts about love that accompanied me on the way to the ridge. These words represent a cyclical process, deepening one's relationship with the Lord. I notice the word Jesus has written in the sand: "love." Basking in the presence of unconditional Love, I open my heart to receive, experience, and accept more of his love. Only then does it become truly extravagant.

Scripture

"[The Lord said,] 'With age-old love I have loved you;
so I have kept my mercy toward you.'"
Jeremiah 31:3

Reflection

1. We all strive to love well, but can you recall a time when you experienced a love that felt unconditional or extravagant? Take a moment to journal that experience, reflecting on how it touched your heart.
2. How do you respond when Jesus says, "Take it in"? Picture yourself in the desert, standing on the ridge with Jesus, and feel his love pouring into you. Allow this imagery to fill you. Capture your thoughts in your journal.
3. Experience through worship. Listen to "Extravagant" by Bethel Music. As you immerse yourself in the song, journal your experience, noting any emotions or revelations that arise in response to Jesus' boundless love.

Day 10

Sandpaper

"We are not destined to happiness, nor to health, but to holiness."

OSWALD CHAMBERS, *MY UTMOST FOR HIS HIGHEST*

We continue sitting quietly on the barren ridge. I would prefer sitting with Jesus on the large rock, where the sand is not as bothersome. However, the radiating heat from the ground is warm and soothing. Jesus seems comfortable, and he gives me the impression that we are not moving anytime soon. Feeling a little squirmy in the sand, I recall a recent conversation with a friend about the benefits of sand. It has valuable qualities, such as scrubbing and exfoliating, which help refine and smooth.

The silence evokes something I heard years ago about "sandpaper people" being put in our lives to help smooth away the rough edges. A crooked smirk crosses my face. Remembering the problematic people that Jesus encountered in his ministry certainly fits the description of sandpaper people. And yet, Jesus loved them.

Love is difficult, and difficult people are hard to love. There are a few people in my life whom I must learn to love, but I often choose complaining, grumbling, and self-pity instead of loving them. Pressing forward in love would mean putting self aside.

I contemplate the sandpaper people in my life who challenge me to love well. I tell Jesus, "I suppose I require more sanding, Lord." He smiles, as he does so often. I lean my head on his shoulder.

Sitting on the ridge, high above the desert floor, I look out over the vast landscape. I call to mind the well-known chapter 13 from First Corinthians on love, and the perfect embodiment of it is Jesus! As we begin our descent from the ridge, I think about the additional sanding and scrubbing I need. Jesus wants my soul to be smoother.

Scripture

"Love is patient, love is kind. It is not jealous, [love] is not pompous, it is not inflated, it is not rude, it does not seek its own interests, it is not quick-tempered, it does not brood over injury, it does not rejoice over wrongdoing but rejoices with the truth. It bears all things, believes all things, hopes all things, endures all things."

1 CORINTHIANS 13:4–7

Reflection

1. Who are the sandpaper people in your life—the ones who challenge your patience and love? Reflect on how you might begin to love them better, despite the difficulties.
2. As you read 1 Corinthians 13, what words or phrases resonate most deeply with you? Take some time to journal about what speaks to your heart and why.
3. Close your eyes and imagine yourself with Jesus as he gently brings to mind your sandpaper people. What thoughts and feelings arise during this time? Journal your reactions, being open to his guidance.

Second Sunday of Lent

Gospel Verse

"From the cloud came a voice that said,
'This is my beloved Son, with whom I am well pleased; listen to him.'"

MATTHEW 17:5

Day 11

Exposure

"And he departed from our sight that we might return to our hearts and find him there. For he left us, and behold, he is here."

SAINT AUGUSTINE OF HIPPO, *CONFESSIONS*

Jesus takes me for a walk at night. The remote desert sky offers a mesmerizing, awe-inspiring display of God's creation. The desert nights are dark and can bring extreme temperatures that require shelter, but, with Jesus, I don't feel vulnerable or susceptible to harm.

The darkness of the desert reminds me of the photographic darkroom in our home when I was growing up. It had an enlarger, trays, chemicals, and other materials needed to develop black-and-white film. No glimmer of light could enter this room when the negatives were developing, or the emerging photos would be damaged.

The heart may be likened to film, at times hidden in a rigid casing, containing a lot of beauty that is waiting to be exposed. The negatives only become beautiful photographs through a multiple-step process. The first step is always to pry the canister open in the dark and remove the film. Then you can begin developing the film.

I wonder what beauty lies within my heart, waiting to be exposed. Thinking about Jesus' heart, I can barely imagine the fullness of its beauty and love. I want a heart like his, and I want to love as he loves. However, the journey into the heart can be long; it involves peeling back many layers that have accumulated over the years.

Jesus conveys to me, "The heart is good at concealing what it wishes to overlook." I inquire how my heart can develop more fully to love as he loves. He looks at me tenderly and says, "Extend mercy instead of judgment." I ask Jesus if we can sit for a while so I can ponder these words and ask myself where I have been quick to judge.

The beauty of time spent with Jesus is that his merciful love guides us into greater self-awareness. I have a clearer grasp of St. Paul's "fruit of the Spirit": love, joy, peace, patience, kindness, generosity, faithfulness, gentleness, and self-control. (See Galatians 5:22–23.) Jesus tells me that a hidden heart cannot expose the fruit held within. It is a lifelong endeavor to unlock our hearts and practice the fruit of the Spirit.

Unveiling the heart can be painful and time-consuming, but I want Jesus to continue to develop my heart and bring light to its hidden places. He holds my heart close to his, and exposure and healing will occur to the extent I am willing to allow. "Jesus, I trust you will carefully open my heart and develop it, just like film in a darkroom is developed fully. I want all your beauty in me revealed."

Scripture

"In contrast, the fruit of the Spirit is love, joy, peace, patience, kindness, generosity, faithfulness, gentleness, self-control. Against such there is no law."
Galatians 5:22–23

Reflection

1. As you spend time with Jesus, ask him to peel away the layers around your heart. Write down what you experience as Jesus helps you uncover the abundant beauty that resides in your heart.
2. Ask the Lord to highlight a specific fruit of the Spirit that he wants you to receive. Record your thoughts.
3. Close your eyes and spend time with Jesus reflecting on these words from the Gospel of Matthew: "Ask and it will be given to you; seek and you will find; knock and the door will be opened to you" (Matthew 7:7).

Day 12

Infusion

"Contemplation is nothing else but a secret, peaceful, and loving infusion of God, which, if admitted, will set the soul on fire with the Spirit of love."

SAINT JOHN OF THE CROSS, *THE ASCENT OF MOUNT CARMEL*

Time with Jesus brings life into perspective. My dislike for the gritty sand has become a distant memory. It seems as if unimportant things fade away in his presence.

I ponder Jesus being led into the desert by the Holy Spirit after his baptism. Where did he sleep during those forty days? Did he have a place to lay his head at night? Was he cold? Was he free from danger? Perhaps Jesus spent nights tucked away safely in a cave.

Some days, the idea of hiding in a cave is very appealing. The world, at times, can draw too much from us and leave us depleted. I wonder if Jesus ever felt that way too. With all the people he ministered to and all the demands placed on him, taking time away to refresh would have been essential.

Scripture says that Jesus often went alone to pray and spend time with his Father. His example inspires us to find solace in prayer and solitude and to seek renewal in our Father's presence. I envision what it might be like for my soul to receive an infusion from God.

"Come, child. Let's walk." Jesus captures my attention. We get up from the sand and begin walking. He continues, "The road of discipleship is filled with victories and challenges. The disciples who walked to Emmaus felt defeated and confused. They walked with me even though it took them a while to recognize me. Look around at those who are walking alongside you."

Yes, there are others alongside me, but I often forget to look around and see I am not alone. Jesus walks right beside me, as do several companions. Focusing on the distance yet to travel or the difficulty of the journey blurs my vision of Jesus and the companions he has sent. I admit that it is hard to ask for help or take time to rest. Self-reliance is a disservice to oneself.

I continue to meditate on what it's like to spend time alone with God, as Jesus did with his heavenly Father. To sit like a child in the arms of God the Father is to experience love, and this acceptance floods my heart! My spirit is carefree when I remember I am cherished by God, and the troubles, anxieties, and sorrows of the world seem to fade. Allowing myself to be a child in God's arms is like an infusion that fills my innermost being—a spiritual blend of love, restoration, and renewal. God, who is Love, gives life.

There are moments when I realize the importance of taking time for spiritual refreshment, which can be found only in God's presence. Just as Jesus demonstrated, the body, mind, and spirit all need time away from worldly demands. Today, I give myself permission to sit in the cave and receive a spiritual infusion from the One who is always with me, ready to offer rest and renewal.

Scripture

"The Father and I are one."
JOHN 10:30

Reflection

1. Sit quietly for a few moments and reflect on what your body, mind, and spirit need today. What do you notice stirring within you? Write down your observations, paying attention to any specific needs that surface.
2. Compose a heartfelt letter to God the Father, asking him to provide the infusion of nourishment your soul needs. Let your words flow with honesty and trust, expressing your deepest desires.
3. Close your eyes and visualize yourself with God the Father, receiving the infusion of love and strength that you've requested. How does this experience make you feel? Describe the emotions and sensations that arise during this sacred moment.

Day 13

Refreshment

"We must remember that the soul is but a hollow which God fills."

C.S. LEWIS, *THE PROBLEM OF PAIN*

I am thirsty this morning. Without water, succumbing to the elements of the desert is imminent. How is our thirst quenched in the desert, when the desert heat evaporates the little moisture that exists? When traveling through arid land, we must be on the lookout for natural springs or wells, as they are of the utmost importance; the sight of one means life.

"Come to the well," Jesus says. I continue to follow where he leads. As we walk, he calls to my mind a season, years ago, when we had spent time together at the well. It was a time of significant depletion for me—life had left me empty; demands, responsibilities, and expectations had left me physically, spiritually, mentally, and emotionally drained.

The heat of the day is upon us, and the sun is beating down. The heat can be debilitating, or it can bring healing warmth. Jesus leads me to a well in the distance. I sit down while Jesus draws water from the well. He knows I'm thirsty. As Jesus hands me a drink, he says, "Frequent visits to the well are needed. It is a life-giving source." I take a drink and begin to feel the relief of the cool water. A sense of comfort washes over me.

I don't know why I waited so long to come to the well. I know it's a place for refreshment and a place to gather with other disciples where we gain strength. But why did I delay until my thirst had become dire? Why do earthly distractions so easily keep us from coming to the well for a drink? I know, intellectually, that the living waters replenish and sustain; however, my actions speak differently.

Self-sufficiency is what drives us to stay away from the well. The lie of self-sufficiency convinces us that we can do it alone. But self-sufficiency only leaves us thirsty. Jesus reminds me that the living waters are always available; the only thing I need to do is to come and drink.

Our thirst for Jesus must be greater than our thirst for the world. If Jesus took time to drink from the well, so should we. He invites us to come frequently to be refreshed so we can be more like the Samaritan woman in John's Gospel who was transformed by the gift of the living waters and became empowered to go out and share the Good News. (See John 4:4–42.) This is a reminder of the importance of prioritizing our spiritual lives, of taking time to refresh, and allowing God to satiate the hollow of our souls.

Scripture

"Jesus answered and said to her, 'If you knew the gift of God and who is saying to you,
"Give me a drink," you would have asked him,
and he would have given you living water.'"

JOHN 4:10

Reflection

1. What is one obstacle or distraction that is keeping you from spending more time with Jesus? Reflect on how you can begin to work toward eliminating it, making space for a deeper connection with the Lord.
2. Think back to a time when you felt physically, spiritually, mentally, and emotionally depleted. What did you do to find refreshment? Reflect on that experience and its impact on you.
3. Meditate on the account of the Samaritan woman at the well in John 4:4–42, as you may hear this gospel reading during Lent.
4. Close your eyes and imagine yourself at the well with Jesus. What thoughts and feelings arise as you sit beside him? Take a moment to share these with him, expressing your heart openly.

Day 14

Presence

"The most holy and important practice in the spiritual life is the presence of God—that is, every moment to take great pleasure that God is with you."

BROTHER LAWRENCE OF THE RESURRECTION, OCD,
THE PRACTICE OF THE PRESENCE OF GOD

Time appears to govern my life. I feel controlled by time, calendars, and deadlines. There are no clocks to observe in the desert and no timetable dictating what comes next. In the desert, presence takes precedence over all else. Time is not of the essence; presence is. Jesus is present to me, as he always is; now, I focus on being present to him.

Jesus and I continue to spend time at the well. Resting is good; my thirst has subsided, and I feel refreshed. Although the heat of the sun beats down, it feels soothing today. Closing my eyes and soaking in the warmth of the rays, I hear Jesus say, "Receive." His words, like a refreshing breeze, begin to restore my spirit.

I feel satisfied at the well. I realize that the longer I stay away from it, the thirstier I become. There are warning signs that indicate when spiritual dehydration is near: discouragement, anxiety, worry, fear, and self-doubt. I also feel scattered and overwhelmed at these times. I must pay more attention to these signs. Remaining in Jesus' presence will help us stay hydrated amidst the world's challenges. The demands of life can be great, but depletion is a reminder that we cannot stay away from the well for too long.

Lingering with Jesus seems more effortless in the desert. It is just the two of us, and I have fewer distractions. If distractions come to mind, I can see them from a different, better, perspective. I revisit the story of the Samaritan woman in John's Gospel and recall that the longer she lingered at the well in Jesus' presence, the more she realized who he was and how much she needed him. Through Jesus' presence, the Samaritan woman was not just refreshed—she was transformed, and she was emboldened to tell others about Jesus.

Being present at the well is facilitated by our awareness of the holy and omnipresent Lord in our midst. As I ponder how to tap into this awareness more intentionally—regardless of what is happening around me—I realize that interior stillness is a prerequisite.

Many days are left to travel in Lent, but images of what Jesus will endure on the way to Calvary flash through my mind. "I thirst," two of the last words Jesus spoke, weigh on my heart. Their significance is not lost on me. Jesus thirsts for all souls to come to the well of living waters. I, too, want to thirst more for Jesus. I breathe in and ask for the grace to cultivate interior stillness and presence.

Scripture

"The Lord answered: I myself will go along, to give you rest."
Exodus 33:14

Reflection

1. How do you experience the concepts of presence, rest, and receiving? When you are in Jesus' presence, how do you feel? Take some time to describe those feelings in detail.
2. Recall a time when you felt spiritually dehydrated. What steps did you take to find refreshment, and what was most helpful during that period? Write about the experience and how it shaped your spiritual journey.
3. Imagine yourself sitting with Jesus at the well, focusing on cultivating interior stillness. What is this experience like for you? Reflect on the peace or insights that come from this moment of quiet connection.

Day 15

Perseverance

"Let nothing disturb you, let nothing frighten you,
all things are passing away: God never changes. Patience obtains all things.
Whoever has God lacks nothing; God alone suffices."

SAINT TERESA OF ÁVILA

Perseverance lies between our times of refreshment and spiritual nourishment. There will always be seasons of persevering—of pushing through the valley or enduring an uphill climb.

Jesus and I continue to spend time at the well. His presence is a constant source of strength and comfort. I am ready to get up and start moving, but I can sense that Jesus is in no rush to leave. "The lesson of perseverance is a difficult one," he says. I nod my head in agreement. When I am frustrated by persevering in the face of challenges, my inclination is to give up quickly.

We practice perseverance in the uphill climbs—those areas where the Lord asks us to stretch and endure—and in the seemingly unending miles of the valley below. The hills and the valleys can feel unrelenting, and our mind quickly gives in, shouting, *It's too difficult. You'll never make it!*

I confide in the Lord, telling him that some days my work feels like I am pushing a weighted sled uphill. He knows I am struggling and gently reminds me, "You push a sled. I carry a cross. Victory awaits at the top."

Jesus explains to me that he is always by my side, many times carrying me as we journey together to the top of the hill. While I am listening intently, he asks me to find joy in the hardships, for there are always blessings and graces in these seasons, although some are a little harder to find than others. These conversations with Jesus are a source of conviction, comfort, and strength.

Being with Jesus calls to my mind this Scripture passage: "Whatever you do, do from the heart, as for the Lord and not for others" (Colossians 3:23). I pray, "Lord, help me remember that all I do, especially the disposition of my heart and my attitude toward hardship and suffering, is my offering to you. I am sorry for not persevering well through the struggle." It is always easier to reach the destination God has for us when our gaze is fixed on Jesus.

There are times when pushing a sled uphill is necessary to build the reign of God. No matter how challenging it is, it still pales in comparison to the weight of the cross. Developing and practicing perseverance brings the mountain peak into view; resiliency to setbacks pushes us up the final incline. Our perseverance is not in vain. It is crucial to building God's kingdom and fulfilling our purpose.

As I meditate on perseverance, I realize two things. First, these seasons do not last forever. Refreshment often appears when I least expect it—unexpected to me but not to Jesus. He knows precisely when the time is right. And, second, stretches of perseverance will always be a part of life, whether in ministry, relationships, internal battles, or interior growth. Calvary was an uphill climb.

I very much needed today's conversation with Jesus at the well. I lean back on my hands and look up at the sky. To be a disciple of the Lord requires sacrifice, but it's also a privilege. After all, Jesus sacrificed far more than I ever will. I sigh and look at Jesus, acknowledging that I have so much more to learn about perseverance.

Scripture

"Therefore, since we are surrounded by so great a cloud of witnesses, let us rid ourselves of every burden and sin that clings to us and persevere in running the race that lies before us while keeping our eyes fixed on Jesus, the leader and perfecter of faith. For the sake of the joy that lay before him he endured the cross, despising its shame, and has taken his seat at the right of the throne of God. Consider how he endured such opposition from sinners, in order that you may not grow weary and lose heart."

HEBREWS 12:1–3

Reflection

1. Think back to a time when you had to persevere through a challenge. What thoughts come to mind about that particular season? What kept you going?
2. The passage from Hebrews 12 says, "Let us rid ourselves of every burden and sin that clings to us and persevere in running the race that lies before us while keeping our eyes fixed on Jesus." What might you need to rid yourself of?
3. Sometimes, the challenges we faced in childhood can shape how we respond to difficulties later in life. Close your eyes and sit quietly with Jesus. Invite the Holy Spirit to bring to mind a memory of a time when you felt frustrated about a tough situation. As you reflect on this moment, tell Jesus about it and ask him to speak his truth to you. Then, take some time to journal your conversation with him.

Day 16

Holy Reliance

"Just as salt gives flavor to food and light illumines the darkness, so too holiness gives full meaning to life and makes it reflect God's glory."

POPE SAINT JOHN PAUL II, FROM HIS ADDRESS ON WORLD YOUTH DAY, 2002

Yesterday, I was eager to get up and move from the well, but today, I am content to stay put. Some days are better for contemplation, as the heart seems more open and receptive. The well in the desert is a good place for resting. It provides quiet for the racing mind and the busy body. The living waters quench my thirst, and Jesus' presence has a soothing effect. It has taken time for me to get to this point of learning to begin abiding, to let my guard down—to just "be."

The essence of an interior life is to grow in holiness and reflect God's nature to others: his love, mercy, goodness, kindness, and more. I think to myself, *What does it look like to be holy and reflect God's glory?*

The image of the transfiguration comes to mind when Jesus' "face shone like the sun and his clothes became white as light" (Matthew 17:2). Holiness is an inward transformation of one's heart, mind, and soul that becomes outwardly visible. If pursuing holiness creates change in us from the inside out, we are closer to the likeness of Christ. The fruit should be visible.

Jesus says, "It is through your weakness that I am displayed." In 2 Corinthians 12:10, St. Paul says, "For when I am weak, then I am strong." But what does that look like? How can Jesus' strength be the driving force within me?

My mind wanders, as usual, as I try to think about how Jesus' strength is displayed in my weakness. Letting my guard down seems to be a key element. When we detach from self—self-reliance, self-sufficiency, self-determination, self-focus, and self-centered desires—we can shift from self to holy reliance on God.

Jesus says, "Reflecting God's glory and radiance is not an action, but a state of being." That is holiness—the process by which we are increasingly made into God's image and likeness. With greater self-awareness, grace to combat sin, dying to self, and holy reliance, less of me and more of Jesus is visible—his strength included.

I lean my head on Jesus' shoulder and close my eyes. I have much to consider. A song from many years ago, "The Fragrance Prayer" by Tom Booth, surfaces. One of the verses says, "Dear Jesus, flood my soul with your spirit and your love. / Penetrate and possess my being so utterly that all my life may only be a radiance of you." Reliance on the Lord in every aspect of life leads to the radiance of God as we surrender, trust him, and love him. It is self that prevents holiness and self that obscures radiance.

Scripture

"Therefore, I am content with weaknesses, insults, hardships, persecutions, and constraints, for the sake of Christ; for when I am weak, then I am strong."

2 Corinthians 12:10

Reflection

1. Think back to a time when you felt you lacked strength. How did you respond at that moment? Can you now see where Jesus' strength may have been at work, even if you didn't recognize it at the time?
2. How is God calling you into deeper holiness? Where might he be inviting you to reflect more of his glory in your life? Take a moment to consider these questions and listen for his guidance.
3. Picture your heart and then ask Jesus to flood it with his love, allowing divine love to radiate and penetrate the deepest recesses of your being. Journal the emotions and insights that arise from this powerful experience.

Third Sunday of Lent

Gospel Verse

"[The Samaritan woman said to Jesus,]
'Give me this water so that I may not be thirsty.'"

JOHN 4:15

Day 17

Stillness

"In the inner stillness where meditation leads, the Spirit secretly anoints the soul and heals our deepest wounds."

SAINT JOHN OF THE CROSS, *THE COLLECTED WORKS OF ST. JOHN OF THE CROSS*

"Be still and know that I am God!" (Psalm 46:11). It is such a simple verse, yet these eight words are quite challenging. In the midst of a bustling season of life, I often find myself reaching for quiet and stillness, only to have them slip through my fingers.

Silence may be more readily available, but stillness demands more. It's easier for me to be still in the desert, especially when I'm sitting with Jesus. His presence nurtures the practice of quieting my body, mind, and spirit. I've come to realize that the Lenten desert provides the graces to practice stillness, to draw near to Jesus, and to look within. With fewer distractions and noises, my heart opens further.

Being still brings both comfort and unease. It offers the space to be introspective and connect with the depths of my heart. The heart, a storehouse for memories and emotions, is a place where blessings—compassion, sympathy, kindness, charity, and mercy, to name a few—can find a home. However, the heart can also hold burdens, such as anger, resentment, envy, sarcasm, and so on. This prompts me to question honestly what is in my heart. And what do I wish to store there?

Jesus recalls Scripture passages about the heart: "With all vigilance guard your heart, for in it are the sources of life" (Proverbs 4:23). "Blessed are the clean of heart, for they will see God" (Matthew 5:8). "For where your treasure is, there also will your heart be" (Matthew 6:21).

I take time to meditate on these passages, to pray, and to ponder. Silence is required to listen, but stillness is necessary to dig deeper and unearth what is hidden within us. Stillness requires dedication, surrender, and, above all else, humility, to cultivate a more profound connection with our heart. Jesus gently helps me continue to delve into what lies inside me. He reminds me to offer myself kindness and grace, which I often forget to practice.

As we stay at the well, stillness of mind and body ensues; both are necessary to "anoint the soul," as St. John of the Cross says. Jesus calls to mind a familiar verse: "You shall make and keep yourselves holy, because I am holy" (Leviticus 11:44). He is inviting me to *be* holy and not to *do* holy. The former is rooted in stillness; the latter in striving. Both are needed to build God's kingdom; however, time spent in stillness, in the presence of God, prepares and fills my soul to do his will and carry out his work.

Through silence and stillness, our heart can more easily hear the voice of God, receive what the Father wishes to give, be healed, and be anointed to go out and radiate his love. The urge to *do* something prods me, but Jesus asks for stillness: "Take this quiet and stillness with you today."

Scripture

There are several passages from Scripture in today's reflection. Pick one that connects with your heart and meditate on it.

Reflection

1. How do you experience silence and stillness differently? Spend time reflecting on this.
2. Ask Jesus to show you what is stored in your heart. Draw a picture of your heart, illustrating both the areas full of joy and the areas that need attention. Take a moment to praise and thank God for the blessings. For the areas that need attention, ask God the Father to help heal them. Be sure to record your thoughts and feelings. (Additionally, consider celebrating the sacrament of reconciliation and let its graces aid you in removing these negative aspects.)
3. Close your eyes. In the silence and stillness, what do you hear the Father say to you, his beloved? Journal your experience.

Day 18

Being

"What a person is before God, that he is and no more."

SAINT FRANCIS OF ASSISI

Jesus gets up from the well, and I follow. It is time to begin walking again. The time of rest at the well has been enlightening and refreshing. I am now learning to appreciate the vastness of the desert and its constancy, which offers few distractions. As we walk together, peace is everywhere—a gift of God's grace.

With each step, though, my mind starts to wander. Lost in thought, a nagging feeling surfaces, a vexing question: *Am I enough*? The world seems to measure worth by what a person has done, performed, accomplished, or accumulated. "Doing" is more straightforward and easier to track, and it feels productive and gives a sense of worth—at least from the world's point of view. The struggle between doing and being is a perennial one.

I ask Jesus, "Why is it such a struggle to *be*? Why do I seem to prefer this life of doing, which frequently carries restlessness and weariness?"

"The mind overcomes the heart," Jesus says.

"The mind overcomes the heart." I repeat the phrase slowly as I take in his words. Jesus' words are few, but their effect is profound.

The innermost desire of a person's heart is to be: to be loved, to be accepted, to be cherished, to be heard, to be at rest. I recall St. Augustine's words in *Confessions*, "You have made us for yourself, and our hearts are restless until they find rest in you." I wonder, *Lord, if I am made for you, why is it so hard to be and to rest with you?*

The dichotomy of "to do" and "to be" continues to nag me. Perhaps I have come to believe lies that question my worth and are fueled by an overactive mind. *Am I doing enough? Am I valuable enough? Do I have enough? Am I enough?*

These questions float around in my mind as we continue walking. I look at Jesus with sincerity as I attempt to grasp the depth of his words. How often do I let my mind overcome my heart? Jesus takes my hand and looks at me. His eyes are filled with kindness. My mind quiets.

Jesus assures me that my identity and my worth are rooted in being a daughter of God the Father, not in doing, accomplishing, or accumulating. This is God's truth. I breathe deeply, sigh, and feel my heart rest with his presence. Being with Jesus is enough; being a daughter of Abba is enough; being me is enough.

Scripture

"Do not conform yourselves to this age but be transformed by the renewal of your mind, that you may discern what is the will of God, what is good and pleasing and perfect."
ROMANS 12:2

Reflection

1. Is resting difficult for you? Do you tend to overthink, overdo, or overperform? If so, reflect on what drives this behavior and how it impacts your sense of peace.
2. When you think about your identity, does it rest in something other than being a daughter or son of God the Father—such as your career, a title, an accomplishment, or even a failure? Consider how these influences shape your sense of self.
3. Imagine yourself with God the Father. What does he look like to you? Where are you in relation to him—are you near or far? How does being in his presence make you feel? Can you see yourself as his beloved child? Reflect on why or why not and explore the emotions that come up.

Day 19

Endurance

"Out of suffering comes the serious mind; out of salvation, the grateful heart; out of endurance, fortitude; out of deliverance, faith. Patient endurance attends to all things."

SAINT TERESA OF ÁVILA

As I approach the midway point of this Lenten season, I can see a change in myself—from apprehension and uneasiness to introspection and peace. The worries of life have lost their gravity. I am putting my cares in perspective. Time with Jesus brings change.

I wonder how many miles Jesus walked when he was in the desert for forty days. Trekking through the desert is taxing, and my legs feel tired at times. We have traveled a considerable distance since starting this journey, but it is difficult to know exactly how far.

Walking with Jesus does not require anything. I can just be. However, sometimes fatigue creeps in. Jesus suggests we sit down. Sitting somewhere other than the desert floor would be more comfortable, but the desert offers limited options. As we sit in the sand, my mind drifts to Calvary. Jesus' legs must have been weakened from the scourging and feeble from carrying the cross. That level of utter exhaustion is unfathomable. Suddenly, my need for rest falls into perspective.

Jesus endured the unimaginable. I cannot grasp the enormity of the suffering he went through for us, for me. How was Jesus able to continue? How did he not give up? My lack of endurance strikes me squarely. When life gets hard, or when outcomes are not what I anticipated or hoped for, I want to call it quits. Jesus was totally obedient to the Father, even to the point of death. How would we have been redeemed if he had adopted my attitude?

"Because he himself was tested through what he suffered, he is able to help those who are being tested" (Hebrews 2:18). "Weariness teaches endurance," Jesus says.

Sometimes I do not believe in my ability to endure. "Jesus, how did you endure all you went through?" I ask.

"Because of love," he replies.

Perfect love will endure. My heart is remorseful as I gain a deeper understanding of the enormity of Jesus' love for me, a love that will bear all things.

Scripture

"Indeed we call blessed those who have persevered. You have heard of the perseverance of Job, and you have seen the purpose of the Lord, because 'the Lord is compassionate and merciful.'"

JAMES 5:11

Reflection

1. Think back to a time when you had to endure something challenging. What helped you navigate that experience? What carried you through?
2. What blessings or lessons emerged from enduring that challenge? Journal about how this experience shaped you and what you gained from it.
3. What blessings or lessons emerge from this verse: "Endure your trials as 'discipline'.... At the time, all discipline seems a cause not for joy but for pain, yet later it brings the peaceful fruit of righteousness to those who are trained by it" (Hebrews 12:7, 11)?
4. Close your eyes and imagine yourself resting in Jesus' presence. What do you feel at this moment? Journal about the experience, capturing any emotions or insights that arise as you find peace in him.

Day 20

Perspective

"The question is not what you look at, but what you see."

HENRY DAVID THOREAU, FROM HIS AUGUST 5, 1851 JOURNAL

Oh, how even the mind has a mind of its own! I struggle to be quiet and focus on Jesus. Some days are like this, with a flurry of distractions and wandering thoughts. We can easily miss what is right in front of us when we are absorbed in racing thoughts and self-focus. It is easy to do.

Concentrating on my breath, I inhale the Lord's peace and exhale the busy thoughts. With each breath, calmness seeps in, and my perspective shifts from one of diversion to one of being present with Jesus.

As we continue walking, I notice a change: we begin to climb. Recalling yesterday's time with Jesus and our discussion on endurance, I consider how some stretches of the journey are difficult to walk; however, learning is in the process, not in the destination. We walk in silence. Being present to each other outweighs conversation now, and silence is a balm for my soul. We continue to travel uphill.

I have noticed that people have more capacity to persevere and endure than we usually exercise. When life gets difficult, self-indulgence and self-pity appear, and we often respond by giving up. Though demanding, getting through the mirage of defeat and conquering the uphill climb is part of character development and soul refinement. As Scripture often reminds us, the battle is in the mind, and the mind requires renewal.

At the top of the climb, the 360-degree panorama offers an unobstructed vista. Jesus says, "I give a new perspective." Struck by the simplicity of his words, I let them sink in. Climbing from the desert floor and to the top of the hill to experience a different view provides a new way of looking at things, but getting to the top is not easy. It tests my resolve, my discipline, my commitment, and my perseverance, but really it tests my love for Jesus. How far am I willing to climb?

Standing with Jesus and looking out over the vast desert, I think about the times when I've lost my perspective—when circumstances or relationships became too difficult to navigate and accepting defeat seemed like the better option. How do I catch a glimpse of what Jesus sees? Has my self-pity or self-indulgence become habitual? Perhaps I have more resolve to keep going than I realized. I think, *Jesus, the view you provide is so much better than mine.*

You did not give up on the climb up the hill of Calvary. Help me view my challenges from a new perspective and endure whatever climb comes my way.

Scripture

"Think of what is above, not of what is on earth."
Colossians 3:2

Reflection

1. How do you typically respond to setbacks and disappointments? Do you find yourself struggling with self-pity or self-indulgence? Or do other emotions surface when your perspective feels clouded? Take some time to journal about your experiences and insights.
2. In chapter 9 of the Gospel of John, Jesus restores sight to a man born blind. What kind of "spiritual blindness" are you experiencing? Consider where or how Jesus might be inviting you to see things from a different perspective in a specific situation. What might he be showing you in this situation?
3. Close your eyes and imagine yourself with Jesus after overcoming a difficult climb. Picture the view from the top and take a moment to internalize this new, broader perspective.

Day 21

Spiritual Agility

"God does not give us overcoming life—he gives us life as we overcome.
The strain of life is what builds our strength.
If there is no strain, there will be no strength."

OSWALD CHAMBERS, *MY UTMOST FOR HIS HIGHEST*

The footing in the desert is different from walking on solid ground. Solid ground is more predictable, while the sand shifts and hides what lies beneath. Jesus is always near, though, and I can lean on him if needed.

Obstacles seem to show up on our path when we least expect them. They frequently seem to appear out of nowhere and at the most inopportune times. They interrupt my steps, cause me to stumble, and often lead to frustration or discouragement.

Jesus shares a few words with me as we trek through the sand: "Spiritual agility is adaptation and the ability to adjust and move quickly." I ponder agility and think about gymnasts. They are graceful, flexible, agile, strong, and sure-footed. I have always been impressed by their ease in pivoting and their fluency of movement. Whether a gymnast has perfectly executed a routine or has faltered, he or she smiles, adapts, and keep going.

I have never contemplated the idea of spiritual agility. Obstacles on our spiritual path require us to pivot or change course to keep moving forward. We don't want to become stuck or stagnant. Our ability and willingness to shift must be grounded in a relationship of trust, knowing that Jesus will provide what we need to confront and overcome any obstacle.

Having this conversation with Jesus makes me realize that my response to obstacles is usually one of grumbling, stumbling, frustration, and defeat. The apostles and early disciples faced obstacles every day of their ministry. Why would walking with Jesus and doing his work today offer anything different for us?

Jesus wants to impart a new approach to facing obstacles: agility and adaptation. Obstacles will always be a part of the journey and outside our control. Trusting Jesus and having faith in his ways will bring peace. And practicing spiritual agility will help us navigate the obstacles that arise instead of becoming discouraged and giving in to defeat.

The Scriptures about faith being tested and perseverance come to mind. I am learning that spiritual growth ensues more in persevering than in reaching a destination or desired outcome. The goal is to keep going when faced with obstacles, not to be overcome by them.

Developing spiritual agility and learning to react to obstacles with adaptability will require much grace. Jesus tells me, "It is with much less consternation that one moves along the path with spiritual agility."

Scripture

"Consider it all joy, my brothers, when you encounter various trials, for you know that the testing of your faith produces perseverance. And let perseverance be perfect, so that you may be perfect and complete, lacking in nothing."

James 1:2–4

Reflection

1. Reflect on the quote by Oswald Chambers. Think about a time when the strain in your life led to greater strength. Journal about this experience.
2. Can you recall a moment when spiritual agility would have been beneficial in overcoming an obstacle? How did you adapt or become more agile and determined to navigate through the challenge? Or did a lack of agility hinder you?
3. Close your eyes and picture yourself with Jesus. Spend some time considering how it is possible to move through our struggles and challenges with joy.

Day 22

Gratitude

"Jesus does not demand great action from us but simply surrender and gratitude."

SAINT THÉRÈSE OF LISIEUX,
STORY OF A SOUL: THE AUTOBIOGRAPHY OF ST. THÉRÈSE OF LISIEUX

Though initially hesitant to heed Jesus' call, I now find my heart overflowing with a deep sense of gratitude for the desert journey. While the desert may appear barren and unremarkable, it mirrors the all-too-familiar routines and mundane aspects of everyday life, where practicing the art of gratitude is essential.

Contemplating the opportunity I would have missed had I declined this Lenten invitation, I wonder how many other invitations from Jesus I have disregarded. Did I overlook them out of selfishness or a lack of wisdom or courage? Was I distracted? My heart is filled with thankfulness that our Lord is persistent. He never tires of drawing us further into relationship with him.

The phrase "attitude of gratitude" stirs in my mind, reminding me that gratitude deserves more attention in my life. Scripture is rich with verses on gratefulness and thanksgiving, a clear indication of its importance in our faith lives. However, we can transform our attitudes only when we actively cultivate a daily practice of changing our old ways.

Jesus begins to speak, and I listen intently: "Gratitude is a condition of the heart. What is your heart bent toward?" I ponder this, asking myself where my heart truly leans. Does it gravitate toward discontent, or does it chase worldly desires, overlooking God's abundant blessings? Perhaps it echoes the fall from grace of our first parents, Adam and Eve, who sought something other than God's abundant love, goodness, and truth.

Life's distractions often entangle us, obstructing our view of God's goodness and generosity. The presence of greed and pride surfaces to the forefront as I acknowledge times when I've prioritized my wants and my will over God's instead of being grateful for his blessings. Cultivating gratitude redirects my focus from perceived scarcity to God's overflowing gifts.

In every situation, we have a choice: gratitude or ingratitude, generosity or selfishness, humility or pride. Although we can't always control our circumstances, we can control our responses. Spending time in conversation with Jesus can illuminate areas where growth is needed, fostering greater self-awareness and spiritual development. It is hard to ask the Lord,

"What needs illuminating?" Pruning can be painful; however, it brings forth new growth and true freedom of the heart, mind, and body, and isn't that what we all really desire?

The lessons of perspective and spiritual agility previously discussed will help me adjust my heart's tendencies. These lessons from Jesus help foster a heart grounded in surrender and gratitude, resilience against life's turmoil, and steadfastness in the Lord.

Scripture

"Give thanks to the LORD, for he is good, his mercy endures forever."
PSALM 118:1

Reflection

1. What invitations from Jesus have you possibly overlooked in the past? What held you back; for example, fear, distraction, comfort, or doubt?
2. Think back to a time when it was hard for you to find gratitude. Write down your thoughts about that experience.
3. How does your understanding of "surrender" evolve as you consider it in light of gratitude? What might Jesus be inviting you to surrender today?
4. Consider three practical ways you can nurture a spirit of gratitude. As you reflect, listen for any insights Jesus may be offering during this time.

Fourth Sunday of Lent

Gospel Verse

"[Jesus said,] 'I am the light of the world. Whoever follows me
will not walk in darkness,
but will have the light of life.'"

JOHN 8:12

Day 23

Sandstorms

"This storm is you. Something inside of you. So all you can do is give in to it, step right inside the storm, closing your eyes and plugging up your ears so the sand doesn't get in, and walk through it, step by step."

HARUKI MURAKAMI, *KAFKA ON THE SHORE*

Sandstorms appear out of nowhere in the desert. They are entirely unexpected and leave little time to prepare. As the wind gathers speed, the sand and debris begin to swirl, visibility dwindles to almost zero, and shelter is essential. It's likely that Jesus encountered sandstorms in the desert.

Years ago, I visited a beach known for its strong winds that was a favorite of kite-surfers. One day, the winds quickly picked up with such force that I became slightly alarmed. Looking down the shoreline, all that was visible was a wall of swirling sand. The grains began to pelt against my skin, and I had to seek cover until the storm passed.

One of the beauties of the desert's expansive landscape is its unobstructed view, which allows us to see for miles. Deserts and mountaintops offer unique clarity, altering our perspective when we view a situation from these vantage points.

Standing with Jesus, gazing out at the desert, I catch a glimpse of what seems to be a sandstorm. In the distance, the clouds of dust are swirling. Jesus and I stand miles away, but we can still feel the peripheral effects of the wind and the blowing sand. Being with Jesus gives me a profound sense of security. I am safe with him; he is my unwavering shelter in the storm.

I ask, "Lord, I don't understand. Why the storms?"

Jesus explains, "Storms are unavoidable. You will walk through some of them, some will remain at a distance, and others will require you to take shelter. Sufficient grace is given for each storm."

Life's storms appear when you least expect them, like the sandstorm I experienced years ago on the beach. Sometimes, we cannot escape life's storms and the stinging effects of the pelting sand.

The Gospel of Mark recounts the story of Jesus' disciples, seasoned fishermen who grew up on the water, caught in an unexpected storm. (See Mark 4: 35–41.) It must have been severe, with winds, swells, thunder, and lightning, to unnerve and terrify these experienced seamen. When they cried out to Jesus, he immediately calmed the winds, and the water also became calm. In silencing the physical storm, Jesus also calmed the interior storm of the men's fears to give them courage. Without courage, we cannot face the storms.

Looking at Jesus, I realize that navigating through life's storms becomes more manageable when we are firmly rooted in faith and believe that he is with us. Jesus reminds me that he is my guide and shelter in the storm. He can calm the storm at any moment, but sometimes we are asked to walk through them. The constant is his grace, and it is more than enough to walk us through the winds and the pelting sand. Fear is always overcome by faith; faith and fear cannot coexist.

Scripture

"The* Lord *is good to those who wait for him, a refuge on the day of distress, taking care of those who look to him for protection."

Nahum 1:7

Reflection

1. Think about a time when you faced a difficult situation, like a metaphorical sandstorm, in your life. How did you manage to get through it? Did you try to handle it on your own, or did you rely on Jesus? Write down your thoughts and experiences.
2. Where is the Lord calling you to have greater faith and trust in him? Journal your insights and feelings.
3. Close your eyes and imagine the Lord with you in a past storm or a current one. What does he want you to know? Can you find rest in him? Take some time to journal about this experience.

Day 24

Horizon

"The horizon leans forward,
offering you space to place new steps of change."

MAYA ANGELOU, "ON THE PULSE OF MORNING"

Jesus and I continue to move through the desert. Although the desert landscape offers little diversity, the mundane often provides the most significant opportunities to learn and grow. Occasionally, we take moments of rest to sit in the sand and observe. Yesterday, the effects of the sandstorm limited our visibility. Today, we can see the long-distance views of a clear desert day.

I look at Jesus, who is gazing at the miles of desert in front of him; turning my eyes from Jesus to the horizon, I ponder for a few minutes the vastness of the desert, which seems to stretch endlessly until the earth and sky blend—the horizon. The horizon was critical to early sailors as a visual boundary that helped them navigate their course.

Concerns begin to creep into my mind, and thoughts of my responsibilities consume me; the vista of the horizon fades. I wonder if Jesus had days when he felt overwhelmed by life and all its obligations—the countless people needing him, the teachings that often fell on deaf ears, the numerous requests for signs and miracles. Was it ever too much, or did he maintain perspective on what was important? That word, "perspective," rings loudly. Determining the relative importance of some things in life compared to others is a struggle we all face.

I stare down at the coarse sand and rocks beneath me and inspect individual grains of sand. My focus becomes like a microscope, zeroing in on the minutiae. While fixating on the grains of sand, keeping sight of the horizon is impossible. Jesus gently lifts my chin and helps me redirect my gaze. I ask, "Lord, how will I keep up if I don't look at all the details?" I struggle to look up, but I bury myself again in the grains of sand.

The expression "Don't sweat the small stuff" rings true. Again, Jesus gently lifts my chin to help redirect my gaze toward the horizon—this time, I allow him to change my view. The horizon holds both the sunrise and the sunset: the hope that welcomes every new day with grace and mercy, and the rest and closure that accompanies the end of each day.

Jesus says, "Where to focus? The choice is yours." I reflect on my need to redirect and look outward. I look at Jesus and feel his love and concern for me. His guidance is a constant source of reassurance and support. The horizon, where the desert meets the sky, where the opaque meets the translucent, where the heavens meet the earth, reminds us that navigating with Jesus is easier than charting life's turbulence alone. Losing sight of the horizon is a sure way to lose our way.

Scripture

"He has marked out a circle on the surface of the deep
as the boundary of light and darkness."
Job 26:10

Reflection

1. Are there areas in your life where you feel overwhelmed? Do you often get caught up in the small details and feel bogged down by them? Take a moment to reflect and record your thoughts.
2. Where might Jesus want to help you gain a new perspective? How can he assist you in looking differently at the challenges you are currently facing?
3. Close your eyes and imagine yourself standing with Jesus, looking out at the horizon. What does he want you to notice and appreciate?

Day 25

Time

"The secret of happiness is to live moment by moment and to thank God for all that He, in His goodness, sends to us day after day."

SAINT GIANNA BERETTA MOLLA, FROM A LETTER TO HER HUSBAND, PIETRO MOLLA

It is said that timing is everything. Keeping a tight calendar, accounting for every hour, and scheduling precisely to maximize each day denotes some level of successful planning. And yet, nonetheless, time escapes us. Perhaps time will always elude us, for it was never ours in the first place.

I reflect on the pace of life and often wish that somehow it would slow down. But the days pass quickly and turn into weeks, months, and years with only highlights that pepper my memory. Time rushes past like a river after a rainstorm. As much as I try to control time, it instead controls me. Governed by deadlines, constraints, targets, and commitments, time slips by.

In the desert, though, time seems inconsequential. Jesus and I walk together and make time to sit and rest. Aside from the rising and setting sun that defines each day, time has little effect on desert life. It is a welcome change and a respite.

The fast pace of life in the world starkly contrasts with the quiet peace of the desert. What is it that slows time and provides tranquility—is it the desert, or is it intentionally walking with Jesus? He is always walking with me, but, I must confess, I sometimes forget. "Better is one day in your courts than a thousand elsewhere" (Psalm 84:11) stirs in my heart.

I reflect on this theme of time and realize that the Lord's time is independent of any parameters we create. Try as we might to be timekeepers, it escapes us. Wanting to dictate time yet losing track of it reveals that we have something more to release. Maybe loosening my grip and releasing time into the hands of Jesus will be more effective. As we continue to sit in the sand, I wait for insight from the Lord. He is quiet and looks out over the wilderness. Jesus squeezes my hand, a reminder that he is near.

Grasping at time has left me tired, dazed, and without peace. Jesus tells me that I want to control what is not mine to control. Apart from Jesus, the constructs of time will govern us. With him, we will be guided in peace and more accepting of what each day brings.

I close my eyes and make an intentional offering to surrender the day and the hours it contains. It takes tremendous energy to hold on so tightly. After releasing my hold on time, I begin to feel freed of its weight, and I lean back and rest in the sand.

Scripture

"For everything there is a season, and a time for every matter under heaven:
a time to be born, and a time to die;
a time to plant, and a time to pluck up what is planted;
a time to kill, and a time to heal;
a time to break down, and a time to build up;
a time to weep, and a time to laugh;
a time to mourn, and a time to dance;
a time to throw away stones, and a time to gather stones together;
a time to embrace, and a time to refrain from embracing;
a time to seek, and a time to lose;
a time to keep, and a time to throw away;
a time to tear, and a time to sew;
a time to keep silence, and a time to speak;
a time to love, and a time to hate;
a time for war, and a time for peace."

ECCLESIASTES 3:1–8, *NEW REVISED STANDARD VERSION*

Reflection

1. What activities or distractions in your life take time away from intentionally walking with Jesus? Reflect on these and consider how they impact your spiritual journey.
2. Choose a verse from the Scripture passage. What message does it convey to you, and how do you feel God is asking you to apply it in your life?
3. Call to mind the story of Lazarus (John 11:1–44) in preparation for Sunday's Mass, when this gospel may be proclaimed. The theme of time is woven throughout these verses, from Jesus waiting to go to see Lazarus, to Lazarus' death, to his being brought to life. What does the Lord want you to glean about his timing?
4. Close your eyes and rest in Jesus' presence. Allow him to guide you in setting time aside for your spiritual growth.

Day 26

Time, Revisited

"The only way of catching a train I have ever discovered is to miss the train before."

G.K. CHESTERTON, *TREMENDOUS TRIFLES*

Do you ever feel the tension between your time and the Lord's time? While time, an earthly construct, dictates our daily lives, it shouldn't constrain how we live for God. Reflecting on yesterday's meditation and Scripture about time, I seek to reconcile this tension between the Lord's time and mine. Releasing control of time is a step toward living in accordance with God's plan. Jesus and I rise from the sand, sharing a smile with one another that transcends words.

Jesus reminds me of a particular afternoon when I had a detailed list of tasks. It was a rainy day, perfect for tackling my to-do list, but the Lord had other plans. As I drove toward home, I saw a homeless woman walking in the rain, carrying her belongings in two trash bags and wearing old sneakers with the heels flattened like slippers. I heard the Lord say clearly, "Give her your shoes."

Surprised, I asked, "Are you sure, Lord?"

He repeated, "Give her your shoes."

I sighed and replied, "OK."

I got out of the car and approached her slowly. She backed away—likely a learned response to strangers. I said hello and asked if she might need some shoes. She declined. I insisted and pressed, but she refused again. *Well, Lord, now what?*

I asked her if she needed anything, and she responded, "Some lunch would be nice." I invited her into my car, loaded her belongings, and spent the rest of the afternoon with her, chatting and grocery shopping, before finding a nearby hotel for her to rest.

Words from Scripture—"Nor are your ways my ways" (Isaiah 55:8) and "Whatever you did for one of these least brothers of mine, you did for me" (Matthew 25:40)—echoed in my mind that afternoon. I had my plans, but God's grace allowed me to hear his voice and release control of what I wanted for that day.

Releasing time to Jesus and allowing space for him to work requires trust. Surrendering our ways and trusting him enable us to fulfill his will each day. The Lord provides ample time for what we truly need to do, and living contrary to his timing leaves us anxious, stressed, and missing the present moment.

Jesus and I continue our walk, enjoying each other's presence. Life is far less stressful when time does not own us. Being held by time or any other stronghold keeps us from experiencing the freedom Jesus intends for us. I thank him for this awareness. I acknowledge that my grip on time will tighten again, and I ask the Lord for the grace to surrender, release, and trust.

I can feel the Lord's peace drawing me deeper into an awareness of his presence. He gently reminds me that he is always with me—unchanging and ever near.

Scripture

"My son, give me your heart, and let your eyes keep to my ways."
Proverbs 23:26

Reflection

1. As you reflect on the theme of time from today and yesterday, ask yourself if the Lord provided opportunities that you struggled to embrace because you felt rushed or pressed for time. Journal your feelings about these moments and consider their potential impact on your life.
2. When have you sensed the Holy Spirit prompting you to change your plans? How did you respond, and what was the fruit of that surrender?
3. What does the Lord want you to understand about "his time"? What is Jesus teaching you about surrendering to "his ways"?
4. Close your eyes and imagine sitting with Jesus. Can you release your concerns about time to him in exchange for his peace?

Day 27

Resistance

"This is a serious warning cry: Surrender without reservation to the Lord who has called us. This is required of us so that the face of the earth may be renewed."

SAINT TERESA BENEDICTA OF THE CROSS (EDITH STEIN), FROM A MEDITATION WRITTEN FOR EPIPHANY, 1941

My mind jumps from one thing to another in seconds, racing from ideas to daydreams to to-do lists to countless other distractions. Although I am physically sluggish today, and my words are even slower to form, my overactive mind makes up for both.

When struggling to connect with Jesus amidst the world's noise, we must exercise dedication and intentionality. Often, I am challenged to enter the quiet space Jesus has set aside for me. Focusing on breathing—inhaling peace and exhaling wandering thoughts and distractions—helps my mind begin to calm. Closing my eyes, I observe that Jesus lovingly waits.

The sand is warm. The heat captured by the desert floor radiates and envelops me. Cupping the sand in my hands, I feel it sift through my fingertips. Jesus invites me to continue our walk in the desert, but my spirit seems reluctant. Apprehension and a touch of stubbornness have crept in. I feel heavy with procrastination. With great effort, I get up from the desert floor. In obedience, I begin putting one foot in front of the other.

I am reminded of many occasions when Jesus has asked for more from me—more surrender, more trust to step out of my comfort zone and embrace seasons of growing in faith. What was my initial reaction in these moments? Did I balk? Did I reject or accept the invitation?

Yes, I often resist when Jesus asks me to stretch and grow. I ask myself, *Why?* Because stretching and growing require more obedience; they require me to be open, to look at the root of my resistance, and to face doubts and fears. Spiritual growth requires us to have hearts willing to accept that they need healing. And, admittedly, healing can be quite difficult.

I look at Jesus. I don't want to be resistant. I don't know what my unwillingness is about. My mind wanders again. Avoidance is a handy tool when we want to escape looking deep within. "Resistance causes delay," Jesus says to me. That rings true. I do not want to delay what the Lord is doing, yet the nature of my resistance is unclear. Eventually, I acquiesce to Jesus' invitation.

Acquiesce. Therein lies the root of my resistance. It is a disposition of the heart, and although I eventually say yes to Jesus, it is colored by my initial resistance, grumbling, and sense of being inconvenienced, and maybe some doubt and fear. Quite simply, what Jesus asks is often difficult. Conviction follows my realization that my heart's disposition and my mind appear to be guided by selfishness. Sometimes, we forget what a privilege it is to serve. *Lord, forgive me.*

As our love for the Lord grows, combating resistance and yielding in obedience to him become easier.

Scripture

"I am grateful to him who has strengthened me, Christ Jesus our Lord, because he considered me trustworthy in appointing me to the ministry."

1 TIMOTHY 1:12

Reflection

1. Describe a time when you felt resistant or reluctant to accept an invitation from Jesus. What were your thoughts and feelings during that moment?
2. Take a moment to connect with your heart. If you find that you struggle with resistance, ask Jesus to reveal the root cause. How does he want to help you remove that root? Journal your reflections and, if needed, offer Jesus your confession. If you haven't already, this might also be an opportunity to seek the sacrament of reconciliation.
3. Close your eyes and sit quietly with Jesus. Receive the grace and truth he has for you, allowing it to fill the space in your heart that used to hold resistance.

Day 28

Temptation

"He did not say, 'You will not be troubled—you will not be tempted—you will not be distressed.' But He did say, 'You will not be overcome.'"

JULIAN OF NORWICH, *REVELATIONS OF DIVINE LOVE*

Temptation always seeks to cause trouble. Enticement, distraction, and allure are all tactics to draw us away from God, away from what is good and holy. Jesus is no stranger to the world's ways and its influence on our thoughts and actions. After all, he spent forty days in the desert at the start of his ministry, experiencing temptation in all the ways we do.

Jesus and I walk together in silence, and the sounds of the desert surround us as gentle breezes shift the sands, occasional sliding rocks begin their descent, and the songs of desert birds fill the air. Time in the desert has provided clarity as I ponder many themes. The quiet and peaceful nature of the desert allows me to reflect more deeply on my thought patterns and behaviors.

Temptation often presents itself in ways that are difficult to recognize. For instance, the temptation to procrastinate when we should be working, or the temptation to speak unkindly when we are angry. That is how the enemy works—discreetly. Temptation will hit where vulnerability exists. Jesus and his disciples experienced many temptations; why wouldn't we expect the same? But is there a way to start identifying these specific temptations before they cause us to stumble?

I recently agreed to an opportunity that, at the time of commitment, made me feel excited and energized. However, today I feel rather disinterested and am struggling to find the fortitude to fulfill the responsibility joyfully. Upon further investigation of my disinterest, I find feelings of avoidance at the surface, but they conceal deeper emotions.

Temptation lures us in. We hear a whispered lie—nobody cares, things will go wrong, no one appreciates this, it won't be successful, and so on. Assaulted with lies and the emotions that follow, we are easily deceived and soon find ourselves in a state of lethargy and idleness. The enemy sees a vulnerability and pitches lies. The false belief or narrative quickly intensifies, and we stop living fully in the freedom Christ has offered us. But we have a choice.

As much as I wish to skirt my commitment, I look deep within to hear the voice of God, which encourages me and reminds me of perseverance and fortitude—even through my feelings of inadequacy. By leaning into God's strength, not mine, the enemy does not prevail. I find that when I turn to God in prayer and Scripture, his strength becomes my own. "[The Lord said,] 'My grace is sufficient for you, for power is made perfect in weakness.' I will rather boast most gladly of my weaknesses, in order that the power of Christ may dwell with me" (2 Corinthians 12:9).

As we continue to walk at a casual pace, Jesus fills my heart with peace. "It is good that we are here," he says.

I am reminded that spiritual and physical commitments require us to sacrifice our desires for God's greater good. Saint Leo the Great said in one of his Lenten sermons, "For there are no works of power...without the trials of temptations, there is no faith without proof, no contest without a foe, no victory without conflict."

I pray, "Lord, guide me as I spend today where you have called me to serve, increase my self-awareness to see the temptations, and fill my heart with your love so that what others see is you."

Scripture

"I have told you this so that you might have peace in me. In the world you will have trouble, but take courage, I have overcome the world."

JOHN 16:33

Reflection

1. What are the temptations you regularly encounter? Take some time to reflect and write down your observations.
2. Can you identify any false beliefs or misconceptions that arise when you face these temptations? Be honest with yourself as you explore these thoughts.
3. Close your eyes and imagine Jesus addressing these false beliefs and replacing them with his truth.

Fifth Sunday of Lent

Gospel Verse

"[Jesus said,] I am the resurrection and the life;
whoever believes in me, even if he dies, will live,
and everyone who lives and believes in me will never die."

JOHN 11:25–26

Day 29

Waiting

"Waiting time is not wasting time.
Waiting patiently in expectation is the foundation of the spiritual life."

HENRI NOUWEN, *YOU ARE THE BELOVED*

I have heard it said that growth is in the waiting. Patience, strength, perseverance, courage, and faith are all tested in seasons of waiting. Too often, we equate waiting with wasting time or not taking charge of a situation. However, the practice of waiting is active and brings awareness of God in our midst when we listen, see, and experience the holy moments around us.

There is a shift in the air; stillness surrounds me as I internalize this time of waiting. I wait for Jesus, quietly listening as he tells me what direction we will take today. Impatience is a daily battle for me. I like things to happen when I want them to happen, but waiting is an integral part of life that we cannot escape. Waiting is woven into every area, every season, and every stage of life, from beginning to end.

Jesus appears pensive, looking off into the desert. Gazing at him, I wonder what fills his mind. I feel a certain heaviness today as I contemplate the end of Lent and the desert walk. It is a simple exit for me, leaving the sandy, rocky desert and returning to the abundance of the world I left weeks ago. For Jesus, his walk to Calvary had a different outcome.

We start walking. With a heavy heart, I ask Jesus, "How did you cope with waiting and knowing what was to come?"

He looks at me tenderly and says, "There is no other way." The weight with which he utters these words penetrates me to the core. As Jesus awaited the walk to Calvary, he abided in the Father's will, with total acceptance of God's way and timing.

God's way and timing can challenge us. I like to know the plan, to sometimes create the plan, and to have answers to the how, the why, and the when. But a life of faith ceases to be faithful if it needs an explanation to move forward. A life of faith means depending on God to answer the questions in the appropriate way and time; it means surrendering to the waiting.

It occurs to me that Jesus is well acquainted with the aspect of waiting in this life. He waited for the right time to start his public ministry, waited for his followers to believe, waited for the prodigals to come home, waited for the sinners to repent, waited for the appointed time to enter Jerusalem, waited for his impending suffering and crucifixion, waited for his exit from the tomb, and waited for the Holy Spirit to fill his people. Jesus still waits for all of God's children to respond to his call to "come and see." (See John 1:39.)

Sometimes, there is no other way but to patiently endure the season of waiting. Waiting isn't wasteful; it allows time for prayer, encourages reliance on the Father, cultivates acceptance and surrender to what God is doing, offers space for discernment and spiritual growth, and fosters an opportunity to receive God's blessings that accompany every season—even that of waiting.

Scripture

"Wait for the LORD, take courage; be stouthearted, wait for the LORD!"
PSALM 27:14

Reflection

1. How do you typically respond during seasons of waiting? What spiritual growth or insights have these periods brought to your life?
2. Recall a time when you did not wait upon the Lord. What lessons did you learn from that experience, and how might it have been different if you had waited with Jesus?
3. Close your eyes, sit quietly, and wait with Jesus. How can you find comfort and peace in this time of waiting?

Day 30

Pacing

"Above all, trust in the slow work of God."

PIERRE TEILHARD DE CHARDIN, *HEARTS ON FIRE*

As the end of Lent draws nearer, I find myself pondering the mystery of a journey. It can seem so long and arduous at the start, never-ending in the middle, and then, suddenly, out of nowhere, the finish line comes into sight. This sense of anticipation, of the finish line appearing when least expected, is a source of hope and expectation.

Although I have never run a marathon, I can appreciate the importance of pacesetting. Proper pacing is crucial to finishing a race. Running too fast out of the gate will bring burnout long before the finish. Keeping the pace too slow will deplete the reserves. The pace is measured as output over time, and finding the right combination takes practice.

Time in the desert has become rhythmic. Before, I found the landscape monotonous; now, I appreciate its constancy. It has become a conducive environment for sitting, praying, waiting, listening, and learning. Some days, I want to rush the process and arrive at the lesson without first walking the necessary path that unveils wisdom and understanding. But it is the journey with our Lord that brings forth fruit.

As I observe Jesus, I see that he is never impulsive and never seems rushed. His pace is steady and displays a certain cadence, illustrating the peace that resides within him. I want that kind of steady pace, that undisturbed peace. Drawn to the peace that Jesus exudes stirs a longing in my heart.

As a child, I remember playing a game of watching and studying my parents' gait. I would mimic one parent's footsteps and then the other's, ensuring our pace was in sync. Today, I realize that watching and syncing my pace with Jesus is the key to a deeper understanding of his ways, his timing, and living in the peace "that surpasses all understanding" (Philippians 4:7).

I also realize that the spiritual exercise of following Jesus' pace requires focus and practice. Struggling to rush the process and finish the race will reveal that hurrying is futile. Spiritual growth occurs in the experiences, not in crossing the finish line. With the proper pace and time allotted to our journeys, we can take advantage of the spiritual blessings and graces.

Pacesetting is like learning to walk; it is part of the spiritual journey. At first, it was awkward, as I was slightly out of step, even clumsy. Locking my arm with Jesus' makes it easier to keep pace. He nods gently and says, "The closer I am, the easier it will be."

Scripture

"Noah walked with God."
GENESIS 6:9

Reflection

1. As you look back on your time with Jesus in the desert so far, have you discovered any areas in your life where you tend to rush the process? If so, why? What have you learned about the pace he desires to set for you?
2. Read and meditate on the story of Noah from Genesis, chapter 6. What did Noah have to learn in order to accomplish the tasks the Lord set before him? What can you take away from Genesis 6:9 or any other verse in this chapter that stood out to you?
3. Close your eyes. Imagine locking your arm with Jesus' and allowing him to set the pace. How does this make you feel?

Day 31

Tuned In

"O Holy Spirit...descend plentifully into my heart. Enlighten the dark corners of this neglected dwelling and scatter there Thy cheerful beams."

SAINT AUGUSTINE OF HIPPO

As I follow Jesus closely this morning, I can't help but feel the awkwardness in my stride. The sand leaves clear evidence of footprints—they are still evolving in fluidity and rhythm as this journey continues. Learning to keep pace with Jesus is a process that will take time. I find myself looking at Jesus like a child waiting for a parent's affirmation. I think about my need for affirmation.

The closer we walk with Jesus, the more we experience being in step with him and in harmony with the promptings of the Holy Spirit. The Holy Spirit is our guide, teacher, and advocate. It's a continuous effort to block out the world and its noise and tune in to the Holy Spirit. The desert, with its few distractions, makes this task seem more manageable. I want to sharpen my ability to hear the Spirit, knowing it will equip me better for the spiritual journey ahead.

I once heard that listening to the Holy Spirit is like listening to the radio. Between stations, the reception is fuzzy and the words indistinguishable, but the sound is crisp and clear when we are dialed in.

The external noises of the world, busyness, and self-absorption all contribute to the static we hear when trying to listen for the nudges of the Holy Spirit. Jesus reminds me that the world is and always will be filled with what distracts us from the divine.

I am trying to understand the lesson Jesus wishes to share. I tell him, "Lord, I am missing the connection between listening to the Holy Spirit and my need for affirmation that arose today."

Jesus replies, "The Spirit affirms the heart. It is the Holy Spirit that validates."

How many times have I looked for affirmation from the world, for validation from others, instead of waiting on the Holy Spirit? Too often to count, and still counting. Contemplating this question, I am reminded of the Bible passage: "Do not store up for yourselves treasures on earth, where moth and decay destroy, and thieves break in and steal. But store up treasures in heaven, where neither moth nor decay destroys, nor thieves break in and steal.

For where your treasure is, there also will your heart be" (Matthew 6:19–21). This passage reminds us that true affirmation and validation come from our Lord, in his way and in his time. When we seek and accumulate accolades on earth, they will always leave us unfulfilled and wanting more.

Do I want to seek temporal affirmations and accolades rooted in my insecurities and pride? Or do I quietly choose to wait upon the Holy Spirit to affirm and validate? Humility is not seeking and asking for worldly affirmations but patiently storing "treasures in heaven" by waiting for the Holy Spirit to affirm us. Earthly treasures will expire and will not await us in heaven. Knowing Jesus more intimately, recognizing his voice, and patiently waiting for the Spirit to speak and affirm fills the heart with all it needs. *Fine-tune me, Lord, so that I may hear You with clarity!*

Scripture

"A clean heart create for me, God; renew within me a steadfast spirit."
Psalm 51:12

Reflection

1. Can you identify situations in which you seek affirmation and validation? How do you typically react when you don't receive the affirmation you desire?
2. Reflect on a moment when you felt affirmed by the Holy Spirit. How did that experience make you feel?
3. Close your eyes and invite the Holy Spirit to speak to you in new and meaningful ways. Listen and take some time to journal your thoughts and reflections on what you hear.

Day 32

Obedient Love

"Love is the root; obedience is the fruit."

MATTHEW HENRY

Hindsight always provides opportunities for introspection. We see how initial apprehension about accepting invitations can give way to grace-filled blessings and consolations.

As I straddled the verdant world and the arid desert, Jesus' invitation to embark on the desert walk began as a struggle. But as time passed, the gift of the desert unveiled my need for spiritual pruning and growth and an opportunity for me to cultivate greater intimacy with Jesus.

Love or obedience: two motivators that compel us to follow Jesus. Obedience alone is motivated by duty to an authority—in other words, compliance. On the other hand, love is motivated by deep affection, devotion, and unselfishness. Love, at times, is asked to surrender, to sacrifice, or to "die to self" for the sake of someone else.

"[Love] bears all things…" (1 Corinthians 13:7). This Scripture surfaces again. I ask myself, *Do I respond out of love or only out of obedience?* I think back to the invitation to enter the desert and admit that I did not meet this invitation from Jesus with a response of love, but rather one of compliance. After weeks of walking with Jesus in the desert, I am convicted by my motivation of compliance, rooted in obedience rather than love.

Obedience, rooted in love, is the model Jesus gives. "And found human in appearance, he humbled himself, becoming obedient to death, even death on a cross" (Philippians 2:7b–8).

I think about the times when Jesus invited me to go deeper into a relationship with him; when he asked for periods dedicated to more prayer, service, and sacrifice; or when he asked me to leave my comfort zone—the safety of the boat—for the waters of the unknown. Often, my response is one of reluctance, peppered with a grumbling spirit. I sigh and whisper to Jesus, "I want to love you more." *Why don't I meet the invitations with love, humility, and gratitude for being asked?*

Transformation of the heart is an ongoing process. Humility heightens our self-awareness, and then the Holy Spirit can illuminate where we need interior work and reveal the hidden areas that need refinement. As I dig further into my response to Jesus' invitation, I realize that fear and ungratefulness lay hidden beneath my response. Had I said no to this invitation, I would have missed out on the beauty of the last few weeks—the time in Jesus' presence, the conversations, the blessings, the lessons, and all the gifts he had in store. Looking at Jesus with remorse, I tell him how sorry I am.

In this moment of conviction, I find myself staring at the ground. Jesus gently asks me to look up at him, but it's hard. The feeling of disappointing him is strong. Yet, amidst it all, I feel the warmth of Jesus' unconditional love. His love is unwavering and unchanging, regardless of my shortcomings.

"Love will come," Jesus says. "These moments are for learning." His gentle words wash over me, and I am filled with gratitude for this revelation. I breathe deeply, look up, and meet his eyes.

Scripture

"For this is love, that we walk according to his commandments; this is the commandment, as you heard from the beginning, in which you should walk."

2 John 1:6

Reflection

1. Recall a time when you followed Jesus' call out of a sense of duty or compliance. What was your attitude during this experience?
2. Reflect on a time when you responded to Jesus out of genuine, obedient love. How did this make you feel, and what was the outcome?
3. Close your eyes and sit quietly with Jesus. Offer him your shortcomings and receive his unconditional love. Take some time to journal your experience.

Day 33

Tug-of-War

"Nothing apart from God can satisfy the human heart, for the heart is truly in search of God."

SAINT ANTHONY OF PADUA, FROM HIS SERMONS

We usually encounter tension between the secular and the spiritual. Worldly allure poses a constant struggle, a battle we all face. If you have followed Jesus for some time, you know the world has elements that always want to tug us away from the sacred. Their empty promise of temporary comfort, wealth, and satisfaction often seems like a tempting escape from life's hardships, disappointments, and losses.

Jesus experienced the allure of the world and all its temptations, just as we do. He was tempted by pride, vainglory, and sensuality. Unlike the frailty of humanity, Jesus exemplified perfect resistance to the tempter and always chose to rest in the strength, encouragement, comfort, and solace of his heavenly Father. Knowing our weakness, Jesus prayed for us: "And now I will no longer be in the world, but they are in the world, while I am coming to you. Holy Father, keep them in your name that you have given me, so that they may be one just as we are.... I do not ask that you take them out of the world but that you keep them from the evil one" (John 17:11, 15).

Our steady pace has brought us miles through the Lenten desert. As I look ahead in the distance, a glimmer of the world to which we will return appears. For now, I am by Jesus' side. *Free will,* I think to myself. *An opportunity to choose, a chance to say yes or no, a decision to draw closer to Jesus or the world.*

Over my years of following Jesus, I have noticed that he never pushes us to say yes. It is a choice we can make; that is the essence of free will—love, and surrender. I ponder the sacrificial love of Jesus and his journey to the cross for the sake of everyone.

I want to follow the path of Jesus without succumbing to the tug of worldly allure. Jesus is always faithful, dependable, and approachable; however, oftentimes, I am not. "Jesus," I tell him, "I don't want to lose sight of you and forget you are here." He looks at me with kindness. Staying close to Jesus is a choice.

As Holy Week approaches, I feel a slight hesitation to continue walking. I want to pause time and remain in the desert. Recalling our Lord's crucifixion makes my heart hurt, and I am finding it difficult to bear the thought of the excruciating pain he underwent for us. It is hard to grasp the depth of Jesus' sacrificial love. I don't think we ever will.

I remain close to Jesus' side and keep my eyes fixed on him. Sometimes, it is easy to look the other way, as many of his followers did. *Holy Spirit, please make me faithful.* I want to instinctively offer Jesus compassion for what he willingly endured. My offering is so small in light of his suffering. I reach for Jesus' hand and quietly walk with him.

Scripture

"Your kingdom come, your will be done, on earth as in heaven."
MATTHEW 6:10

Reflection

1. Today's theme of tug-of-war between the earthly and the spiritual represents the battle between our will and God's. Identify and list some areas in your life where you struggle with this tug-of-war.
2. Ask the Holy Spirit to reveal a recent temptation that led you to sin. Write a heartfelt note of sorrow or repentance to Jesus.
3. Close your eyes and imagine handing Jesus the note you wrote. Wait and listen for his response. Ask Jesus to show you the truth he wants you to understand. Record your experience.

Day 34

Receptivity

"Keep your heart open and remember whose you are."

ANONYMOUS

I first heard this phrase many years ago. These words have resurfaced as I consider what an open and vulnerable heart might look and feel like.

Jesus and I find a resting spot in the desert. We have been walking for a long time now, and it seems like an appropriate time to rest. We sit at the base of a large, dusty cliff where we can lean against the rocks, and I am contemplating the posture of my heart. Does it naturally remain open, or does it have the propensity to be cautious, aloof, or closed? I consider Jesus' open heart, full of love, compassion, and mercy, one that gives and receives. I want a heart like his, but life can cause pain, and pain can create a closed and hardened heart.

When a heart is wounded, it may respond by shutting itself to further injury. For instance, we may close our hearts to feelings and emotions if we've been hurt by harmful words. We may close our heart to meaningful relationships if we've been rejected or abandoned. If betrayed, a once-trusting heart may choose not to trust anymore.

Healing is a journey, and peeling back the layers of a wounded heart is a process that takes time, but Jesus has time and can heal anything we want him to heal. To have a heart like Jesus requires our openness so he can reveal what lies within.

Wounded hearts can lie veiled and hidden, displaying the effects of their hurt through the words and reactions they release. I wonder about my heart and where it may be hurting. I ask Jesus to reveal my wounds, to heal these broken places, and to fill those places with his mercy, truth, and love. Broken hearts can be healed when placed in the hands of the God who heals.

"Remember whose you are" continues to ruminate in my mind. I know I am a daughter of the King, the Most High. It took me many years to accept this truth and open my heart to receive the Lord's love and healing. It is still an ongoing process. Life's struggles attempt to blur our identity as cherished sons or daughters of the Father. However, walking closely with Jesus reminds us "whose we are" and helps keep our hearts from closing.

I want a heart that is fully open to receive all the Lord offers. With an open heart, I realize I risk being hurt by the world. However, people in Jesus' life harmed and wounded him, and that didn't stop him from keeping his heart open and loving and giving completely.

Being in Jesus' presence has filled my heart with more love and compassion in preparation for Holy Week. This Holy Week will be different, as the desert journey has drawn me more deeply into Jesus' heart and given me a more profound understanding of his sacrifice.

Walking toward Good Friday begins to grip at my core. I ache, contemplating the unimaginable that Jesus suffered. But there is hope in the resurrection—the ultimate expression of an open heart that loves unconditionally and wants to give generously. I want to open my heart to receive all the love, grace, and healing that pours forth from the cross.

Scripture

"Ask and it will be given to you; seek and you will find; knock and the door will be opened to you."

MATTHEW 7:7

Reflection

1. How would you describe the current state of your heart? Is it open, receptive, cautious, or something else? Consider spending time before the Blessed Sacrament in prayer. You may also want to go to confession or Mass to allow the Lord's graces to flood your heart.

2. Are you willing to ask Jesus to reveal any hidden wounds in your heart? As he shows you, ask him to uncover the lies you might believe about yourself because of these wounds. Then, invite Jesus to comfort you and replace those lies with his truth.

3. Because the heart "is the place of encounter" (See the *Catechism of the Catholic Church*, 2563.) with God, the Sacred Heart image can help facilitate a heart-to-heart encounter with our Lord. Pope Francis said in his encyclical *Dilexit Nos* (He Loved Us), "More than any other part of his body, the heart of Jesus is 'the natural sign and symbol of his boundless love.'" Close your eyes and spend some quiet time with Jesus. Allow him to fill your heart with the boundless love of his Sacred Heart. Afterward, draw a picture of what your heart looks like now.

Palm Sunday

Gospel Verse

"[Christ] humbled himself, becoming obedient to death, even death on a cross. Because of this, God greatly exalted him and bestowed on him the name that is above every name."

PHILIPPIANS 2:8–9

Day 35

Unreliability

"No pain, no palm; no thorns, no throne;
no gall, no glory; no cross, no crown."

WILLIAM PENN, *NO CROSS, NO CROWN*

Jesus and I are still resting at the base of the cliff. The desert walk has been beautifully challenging and, like most journeys, unpredictable; it has brought ups and downs, joys and sadness, victories and defeats. The one thing I can—we all can—always rely on is Jesus.

As I lean against the rock cliff, I contemplate the Palm Sunday Scriptures, which joyously welcome Jesus into Jerusalem for what begins his walk to Calvary. Followers of Jesus greet him at the city gates, celebrating with palm branches, lining his path with cloaks, and singing, "Hosanna! Blessed is he who comes in the name of the Lord! Blessed is the King of Israel!" Surely, I would have joined the others in singing praises had I been there, wouldn't I?

Reflecting on my commitment to follow Jesus, I imagine myself at the city gates of Jerusalem, watching Jesus pass by. How did we, the people, go from celebrating Jesus with songs of praise, palms, and cloaks to denouncing and condemning him, screaming, "Crucify him! Crucify him!"? What starts as a triumphant journey into Jerusalem quickly changes into one of disdain and spurn. Lord, how can people despise you so much as to spit at, strike, and beat you? I struggle to comprehend such a display of insult and injury toward Jesus. How did we move from honor and glory to blame and persecution? The followers of Jesus include unreliable and fickle people.

It's a stark contrast, isn't it? How easily we move from celebration and exaltation to ridicule and condemnation, from saintliness to sinfulness. In between lies this chasm of indifference or, as Scripture refers to it, being "lukewarm." (See Revelation 3:15–16.) I have found myself on the entirety of this spectrum—from attempted saintliness to lukewarmness to sinfulness.

Participating in such hateful behavior toward Jesus as depicted in Scripture may be hard to imagine today. As his disciple, though, I also realize that my unreliability and unfaithfulness may not be displayed by spitting, mocking, and beating, but through other means. Reflecting further, I ask myself, *Where does unreliability reside in me?* Am I present to Jesus? Do I spend time with him, or do I too easily forget him? Am I patient with others? What unkind thoughts and judgments float in my mind? What harmful words slip out of my mouth? How do I treat my neighbors? Do I neglect my prayer life and Scripture study? Do I gossip or tell white lies? As I look at Jesus, I gain a deeper understanding of the human behaviors that drove the nails.

Jesus waits patiently as I work through this meditation. He signals that it is time to get up and start walking again. We begin the final approach to the desert's edge. I notice that the rhythmic pace we kept at the beginning of this journey has given way to a heavy, more burdensome stride. Our steps have slowed as the cross quickly approaches. I roll my shoulders forward and look at the ground, feeling the gravity of that first Good Friday.

I look at Jesus and ask him, "How did you endure all of this?"

He replies with one word: "Love." But I can already sense it in his eyes. It is hard to fathom this kind of love, a love that is willing to sacrifice reputation, belongings, dreams, desires—everything—to lay down one's life. Saintliness or sinfulness, exaltation or humiliation, love or indifference; these are the daily challenges we face as we walk more deeply in friendship with the Lord. May our desire grow each day to give him more of our hearts. Jesus, help us to love as you love.

Scripture

"That he may grant you in accord with the riches of his glory to be strengthened with power through his Spirit in the inner self, and that Christ may dwell in your hearts through faith; that you, rooted and grounded in love, may have strength to comprehend with all the holy ones what is the breadth and length and height and depth, and to know the love of Christ that surpasses knowledge, so that you may be filled with all the fullness of God."

EPHESIANS 3:16–19

Reflection

1. Read Mark 11:1–10. What strikes you as you read the account of Palm Sunday? How is the Lord challenging you to greater reliability, faithfulness, and love? Journal your feelings and thoughts.
2. Lukewarmness often occurs on our spiritual path. How does this play out in your own journey of faith?
3. Close your eyes and sit quietly with Jesus. Receive his love. Ask the Lord to help you "comprehend with all the holy ones what is the breadth and length and height and depth, and to know the love of Christ that surpasses knowledge" (Ephesians 3:18–19).

Day 36

Battlefield

"Jesus permits the spiritual combat as a purification, not as a punishment. The trial is not unto death but unto salvation."

SAINT PIO OF PIETRELCENA, FROM HIS LETTERS

In the distance, I can see Golgotha, "the place of the skull." Staying close to Jesus and locking my arm with his, I try to consider the immense battle he faced there when his appointed time drew near. He cried out in surrender to his Father from the Garden of Gethsemane, "Not my will but yours be done" (Luke 22:42) as he accepted the walk to the cross.

Jesus is intimately familiar with our struggles and reminds me that he knows well the lure of temptation and the attacks we face on the spiritual battlefield. The battlefield resides in the mind, where the war is won. I contemplate the different mindsets that can occupy my thoughts, like the joyous, confident attitude that makes me believe I can do anything and the deceitful whispers that back me into a dark corner.

On many occasions, I have found myself standing amid the battlefield, dodging the enemy's attacks. Most recently, I recall a bombardment of self-doubt and discouragement. Even though I know the enemy is searching for weaknesses to capitalize on, I still fall for his deception; fighting through one of these onslaughts can be arduous. But I know Jesus understands this struggle. He gives us strength to endure and persevere.

How did Jesus battle what the enemy hurled his way? Jesus faced fierce attacks during his ministry. I can't even imagine the all-but-crushing weight, for the enemy knew that the divine act of salvation hung in the balance. "Jesus," I say, "I can't even imagine how you sustained the weight of the tempter's attacks and oppression. How did you persevere and prevail?"

"You need a strategy to stand firm on the battlefield," Jesus tells me. "Everyone is susceptible to the enemy." Jesus reminds me that the enemy will always offer the earthly satisfaction or the temporal gratification.

Jesus acknowledges that the enemy's attacks can be depleting and demanding but reminds me that I do not battle alone. "I will never leave your side," he tells me. Some battles are won quickly, and others take time. He relays the importance of perseverance and strengthening my will through prayer, fasting, the sacraments, the Scriptures, community, and outreach to others. The battles will help refine and purify my soul and lead me to yield to the will of the heavenly Father.

I wish I could stop and stay where I am with Jesus, but the path through the desert leads to my own "personal Calvary." I want to fast-forward to Easter, to the celebration of the resurrection, but I know there is no Easter without Good Friday, no joy without sorrow, and no triumph without fighting through the battle.

We will soon exit the quiet stillness of the desert to recall the chaos of the crucifixion, when Jesus battled "not unto death but unto salvation," as Padre Pio wrote. Keeping Jesus' sacrificial offering of suffering in the forefront of my mind will help me endure a spiritual battle.

Scripture

"He advanced a little and fell prostrate in prayer, saying, 'My Father, if it is possible, let this cup pass from me; yet, not as I will, but as you will.'"

Matthew 26:39

Reflection

1. As you reflect on today's theme, recall some of the spiritual battles you have fought. How were you able to endure?
2. Is there a particular struggle or challenge to which you can invite the Lord to join you on the battlefield? Visualize this battle and listen to what Jesus wants to impart to you.
3. Close your eyes and meditate on Exodus 14:14: "The Lord will fight for you; you have only to keep still." Allow Jesus to take up the fight on your behalf. Journal your impressions and insights.

Day 37

Outstretched

"Everything is a reminder of the cross.
We ourselves are made in the shape of a cross."

SAINT JOHN VIANNEY

Jesus and I stand at the desert's edge. This time, the edge represents both the end of Lent and the exit from the desert. The whirl of emotions I am experiencing contrasts dramatically with those I felt at the start of this journey. Standing at the edge and looking back, I am filled with appreciation for the hidden treasures in the desert. Little by little, the desert trek unearthed meaningful conversations, lessons, reflection, self-awareness, and spiritual growth. The desert journey cultivated an intimacy with Jesus that has forever changed and deepened my relationship with him.

How did our time in the desert pass so quickly? The forty days have all but come to a close, and the commemoration of our Lord's passion is now here. I consider the Last Supper and Jesus' betrayal, arrest, and scourging. My mind is bombarded by hundreds of images of the crucifixion: Jesus' arms outstretched, nailed to a wooden cross, fighting—not for his life, but for ours.

Oddly, the position that signifies death on a cross resembles the modern-day power pose—a confident stance, with arms outstretched, relaying power, strength, commitment, and authority. The juxtaposition is notable.

As St. John Vianney said, "We ourselves are made in the shape of a cross" in solidarity with our Savior, whose life exemplified sacrificial giving, vulnerability, approachability, mercy, and love. As I look to Jesus, he reminds me that sacrificial living is rooted in unconditional love: the kind that's willing to die to self. Sacrifice builds the reign of God, one offering at a time.

The cross was the instrument for the Son of God to make the ultimate sacrifice. He suffered for my sake and for the sake of all humanity. Through his suffering, sacrifice, and resurrection, death was defeated, salvation ushered in, the relationship between God and humanity restored, and freedom made available to all who wish to receive it.

Scripture

"Jesus answered them, 'The hour has come for the Son of Man to be glorified.'"
JOHN 12:23

Reflection

1. As you contemplate the commemoration of Christ's passion, what emotions or thoughts arise within you? Consider the depth of his sacrifice, the weight of his love, and the pain he endured for our sake. How do these reflections stir your heart?
2. Reflect on your journey through the desert. What moments with Jesus stand out the most? Were there times of solace, challenge, or transformation? How did his presence guide you through these times?
3. Close your eyes. Imagine you are standing at the edge of the desert with Jesus by your side. What words surface within you that you want to share with him? What does your heart long to express? As you listen in the stillness, what does Jesus want you to carry with you as you continue your path?

Day 38

Farewell

(HOLY THURSDAY)

"The pain of parting is nothing to the joy of meeting again."

CHARLES DICKENS, *THE LIFE AND ADVENTURES OF NICHOLAS NICKLEBY*

I have grown fond of the landscape, the arid conditions during my time with Jesus. The desert provides a favorable environment for increased prayer and contemplation; silence and solitude create a space for cultivating love and satisfying the longings of my heart. Saying farewell and parting from this sacred space weighs on my heart.

Like all experiences, the Lenten season has a beginning, a middle, and an end. The start of Lent brought hesitations and doubts; the days in the middle brought insight and self-awareness, highlighting where my heart needed mending; and the end revealed not only my expanding love for Jesus—a love that has grown and deepened throughout this journey—but also a profound sense that I am unconditionally loved.

I want to linger at the desert's edge with Jesus and prolong Lent's inevitable end. However, Jesus reminds me of his mission: "For this I was born and for this I came into the world, to testify to the truth" (John 18:37). The end of Lent is upon us, and today is Holy Thursday, the day when Jesus shared the Last Supper with his disciples and the start of the holy Triduum.

The gravity of Christ's passion descends on me with immense weight. What Jesus endured for our sake is almost beyond comprehension. How can one fully grasp such love, such sacrifice? It is a mystery I will continue to ponder for a lifetime. And yet, even with the shadow of Calvary looming, Jesus took time to share a final meal with his beloved disciples. He broke bread and shared the cup of wine, instituting the first holy Eucharist—an everlasting gift that nourishes and sustains us through every age.

On this solemn Thursday, the Eucharist will be carried out from sanctuaries around the world. This ritual symbolizes the quiet withdrawal of Christ's presence as he prepared for the cross—when his body was broken and his blood poured out for the forgiveness of our sins in boundless love.

All I can do now is sit in the present moment with Jesus, soaking in his love—the very essence my soul longs for. I reflect on the themes of these Lenten weeks: the fears, the doubts, the surrender, and the quiet realizations about his mercy and love. As we sit in silence, there is a sacred exchange, and my heart feels wider, fuller, more receptive. I realize it is beginning to overflow not with my love, but with Christ's love dwelling within me.

As the desert journey comes to a close, Love continues to walk with me.

Scripture

"While they were eating, Jesus took bread, said the blessing, broke it, and giving it to his disciples said, 'Take and eat; this is my body.' Then he took a cup, gave thanks, and gave it to them, saying, 'Drink from it, all of you, for this is my blood of the covenant, which will be shed on behalf of many for the forgiveness of sins.'"

MATTHEW 26:26–28

Reflection

1. As you meditate on the Gospel of Matthew, envision yourself at the Last Supper. Where do you find yourself in this sacred moment? Are you seated close to Jesus, perhaps listening intently to his words, or are you engaging in quiet conversation with him? Notice your surroundings: who is near you, and what do you hear or see?
2. As you immerse yourself in this scene, what emotions, feelings, or thoughts begin to surface? Do you feel a sense of awe, reverence, or perhaps a deep connection with the Lord? Capture the emotions, thoughts, and insights that arise from this visualization exercise.
3. What does this encounter at the Last Supper reveal to you about your relationship with Jesus, and how does it shape your understanding of his sacrifice and love? Take time to journal your reflections.

Day 39

Accomplished

(GOOD FRIDAY)

"O Jesus! You who did not spare yourself to have compassion on me, but did die upon the cross for my sake, save me, and may my salvation be to love you forever."

SAINT ALPHONSUS LIGUORI, *DEATH, JUDGMENT, HEAVEN, AND HELL: MEDITATIONS ON THE FOUR LAST THINGS*

On this day, more than two thousand years ago, darkened skies shrouded the land as Jesus cried from the wood of the cross, "*Tetelestai!*" ("It is finished!") Did the observers even hear him or notice he had spoken? Were they more interested in the spectacle or the One in their midst suspended between heaven and earth?

I am sitting alone at the edge of the desert. It is still and hauntingly silent. The air is heavy, and the heat of the midday sun radiates down. All I can hear is the beating of my racing heart. I think about Jesus' heart on that day; it no longer beats. I imagine myself at the scene of Calvary.

I head to the hill. I begin the walk toward the cross, where Jesus is motionless. There are countless people gathered—many more than I anticipated. As I make my way through the crowd, the cross comes into view. I stop and struggle to keep going. I can see Jesus in the distance. He is unrecognizable. I cup my face in my hands; the tears fall.

With a broken heart, all I can think about is God the Father, on his throne in heaven, watching his beloved Son sacrificed. I also imagine Mary, our Blessed Mother, at the foot of the cross, enduring the unspeakable anguish of an unjust death. The loss of a child—there is no greater pain than that of a parent losing his or her child.

How could *they* have done this? It is a rhetorical question. The answer is clear. "They" are us, and we are all sinful people who need a Savior. A Savior who loves with a love that never fails, a love that never abandons, a love that sacrifices and forgives, a love that heals and restores, and a love that never ceases to pursue us and call us home to the Father.

"For the sake of the joy that lay before him he endured the cross, despising its shame, and has taken his seat at the right of the throne of God. Consider how he endured such opposition from sinners, in order that you may not grow weary and lose heart. In your struggle against sin you have not yet resisted to the point of shedding blood" (Hebrews 12:2b–4).

Jesus' ultimate sacrifice on the cross is the reconciliatory act of forgiveness, healing, and restoration for a wayward people, of which I am one. I see myself kneeling on the rugged, rocky road where Jesus had walked hours before. I look up at the Savior of the world, hanging on the cross, his head bowed down. He breathed his last for you and me. *Forgive me, Lord, for I know not what I do.*

Scripture

"When Jesus had taken the wine, he said, 'It is finished.' And bowing his head, he handed over the spirit."

JOHN 19:30

Reflection

1. Imagine yourself standing at the edge of the desert. Jesus is no longer by your side. What emotions arise within you? Perhaps there's a sense of loss, uncertainty, or longing. Reflect on the experiences and memories that surface in this moment.
2. Consider what you would want to share with Jesus if you were there at Calvary. What thoughts, concerns, or gratitude would you express? What burdens or hopes do you carry in your heart at this sacred destination? Likewise, what would you want to share with the Blessed Mother if you were with her at the foot of the cross?
3. Close your eyes and invite Jesus to speak to your spirit. Open yourself to his presence. What does he reveal to you in this intimate moment? Journal the insights, emotions, and words that surface from this encounter.

Day 40

Silent Tomb

(HOLY SATURDAY)

*"The works of God are marked with silence.
It is in the silence of prayer and retreat, in the silence of the desert
and the forest, that great souls receive their message from God."*

PÈRE JACQUES OF JESUS, OCD,
FROM HIS 1943 RETREAT FOR THE CARMELITE NUNS OF PONTOISE, FRANCE

There were no more cheers and applause, no more scoffing and ridicule coming from the crowds who attended Jesus' crucifixion. It was silent. Only an empty cross remained, inscribed with "Jesus of Nazareth, King of the Jews" in Latin, Hebrew, and Greek. I now visualize myself standing and staring at that vacant cross, remembering Jesus' final words, "Father, into your hands I commend my spirit" (Luke 23:46).

Standing there, I can't help but reflect on my journey of resistance and surrender. How often do I resist commending my spirit to the Father? There is always the option to resist or surrender. Resistance can leave us void of the graces and blessings the Lord has in store. Surrender, the better choice, is accompanied by either a humble and willing heart or a grumbling one. Admittedly, it is often an ongoing challenge to surrender and to do so in joy and humility.

Today, my perspective differs from those who walked away from Golgotha 2,000-plus years ago. Jesus' followers and the spectators believed it was the end—the ministry over, the miracles gone, and the signs and wonders finished. His disciples left Good Friday brokenhearted and crushed in spirit. Jesus, the One they loved, was now gone, laid in a tomb.

On this silent Saturday, I see myself walking away from Golgotha. I head to the tomb where Jesus' body lies. I contemplate the dark, damp space that holds Jesus' body. The cavern holds stillness and silence. But stillness and silence do not mean God is not at work. The most significant work of all, the resurrection of Jesus Christ, was accomplished in a stone-covered tomb. In the dark hush of the cavern, a miracle unfolded.

Likewise, the progression of the interior life is hidden deep within the veiled heart. It is a daily walk of commending our spirit to the Father. The work is done quietly, in the inner sanctum, through prayer, Scripture, sacrifice, sacraments, study, and time spent with Jesus, cultivating an intimate friendship that draws us further into his Sacred Heart. Although the intimacy of our relationship stays hidden in part, the visible fruits of our time with Jesus reveal the transformative nature of his love.

I reflect on how being present with the Lord has brought revelation and healing. Spiritual growth can be slow, arduous, and, at times, painful. It is a process of opening our hearts to the heart of Jesus through building trust, vulnerability, and love. Love has the power to transform everything and everyone.

Tonight, at the Easter Vigil, we celebrate the triumph! "This is the night when Christ broke the prison-bars of death and rose victorious from the underworld" (*The Exsultet*)—the movement from the agony of the cross to redemptive joy. We recall when the tomb was found empty, when darkness gave way to light, and the resurrected Jesus Christ overcame sin and death. I am overwhelmed by joy as we celebrate his resurrection. Most of all, I am eternally grateful for the story of salvation and the Father who loves us too much to leave us where we are. He will never tire of pursuing us, regardless of how far we have wandered. We are never too far away to be found.

We adore you, O Christ, and we praise you, for by your holy cross, you have redeemed the world.

Scripture

"When the Sabbath was over, Mary Magdalene, Mary, the mother of James, and Salome bought spices so that they might go and anoint him. Very early when the sun had risen, on the first day of the week, they came to the tomb. They were saying to one another, 'Who will roll back the stone for us from the entrance to the tomb?'"

Mark 16:1–3

Reflection

1. "Tomb-like" seasons—those periods of stillness, waiting, or loss—are a part of life. Reflect on your own journey through those seasons. What has your experience been during these times, and how have they shaped you?
2. During "tomb-like" seasons, what does the Lord want to resurrect in you? Where does he want to breathe new life?
3. Close your eyes, be fully present with Jesus, and allow yourself to fully experience this moment with him.

Easter Sunday

"We are an Easter people, and Alleluia is our song."

POPE SAINT JOHN PAUL II, FROM THE NOVEMBER 30, 1986, *ANGELUS*

I imagine myself in the pre-dawn hours of that first Easter morning. I head to the garden that holds Jesus' tomb. As the first light emerges, I begin to see the outline of the stone that once blocked the tomb's entrance. The stone is rolled away, for it is no longer needed! As I peer into the tomb, I am filled with elation.

I hear the voices of the women who are approaching. "When the sabbath was over, Mary Magdalene, Mary, the mother of James, and Salome bought spices so that they might go and anoint him.... On entering the tomb they saw a young man sitting on the right side, clothed in a white robe, and they were utterly amazed. He said to them, 'Do not be amazed! You seek Jesus of Nazareth, the crucified. He has been raised; he is not here'" (Mark 16:1, 5–6).

A dark, damp, and empty tomb—God's mightiest work! As I look into the abandoned tomb on this glorious morning, I am filled with indescribable joy. The story of salvation is now ours—a story of pursuit, sacrifice, and redemption. We are children of a heavenly Father who relentlessly pursues us with his love; his love is too great to let us stay unchanged.

Staring at the empty tomb, I am reminded that light penetrates the darkness, death is defeated, sin is conquered, and the crux of our faith, the resurrection of Jesus Christ, is forever etched in our hearts. The Lenten season has ended, and the barren, arid desert—a stark symbol of lifelessness—receives the seasonal rains as the clouds, high in the sky, release their water droplets to baptize the earth. New life begins. The flowing rains spark the hidden life beneath the desert sand. The waters flow, and the streams and rivers emerge. Flowers, grasses, and small shrubs flourish, and the desert garden overflows, providing a bounty of life to all.

We live in the desert rains, where grace flows down from heaven, life is abundant, and our joy has been made complete (See John 15:11.) in the victory over sin and death by the resurrection of Jesus Christ. God's mercies await us every day, and every day brings the possibility of little resurrections as the Holy Spirit breathes new life into the areas of our hearts that long for healing, restoration, and renewal.

We are an Easter people, resurrected sons and daughters, who have encountered the risen Lord. We are not at the scourging or at Golgotha. We are not waiting in the darkness before the silent tomb, nor are we asking, "Who will roll back the stone?" (Mark 16:3). And we are not weeping because "they have taken [our] Lord and [we] don't know where they laid him" (John 20:13).

Alleluia is our song! Alleluia is a song of exaltation, a song of indescribable joy, and a song of praise and thanksgiving. Is it your song? Having shared honestly throughout this desert journey, I admit that it is not always my song. I earnestly want it to be, but sometimes I forget that the One who conquered sin, bought my freedom with his life, defeated death, and loves me unconditionally ushers in, for each of us, Alleluia as our song. Will we claim that song of jubilation, praising what God has done? As C.S. Lewis reminds us in *Mere Christianity*, "He died not for men, but for each man. If each man had been the only man made, he would have done no less." That is how much he loves us!

We have heard the "Good News of great joy that will be for all the people" (Luke 2:10). It comes to all the people only if we choose to live in that great joy. It comes to all the people only if we participate in proclaiming the Good News. It's a daily choice to see the Good News, live the Good News, and share the Good News.

Our mission as an Easter people is to be the sweet song of Alleluia for each person who enters our lives. Let our song fill the air so others may hear and may experience the power of the living God—so that they may be drawn out of the barren, arid desert lands and into new life. Let us "sing a new song to the Lord" (Psalm 98:1) and remember that "this is the day the Lord has made; let us rejoice in it and be glad" (Psalm 118:24).

Scripture

Re-read the Scriptures mentioned in today's meditation as well as John 20:1–9. Spend time reflecting on what you read.

Reflection

1. As you celebrate Easter Sunday, the holiest day in our Christian faith, reflect on your Lenten journey—from the desert, to the cross, and finally to the resurrection. Consider journaling about the blessings, joys, and significant experiences along the way.
2. Which revelation or insight about yourself, Jesus, or your relationship with him was the most impactful during this journey?
3. How can you embody the spirit of Alleluia and bring this joy and hope to those around you?
4. Close your eyes and spend time in the presence of the risen Lord. Consider how you might continue this style of prayer with the Lord throughout the year. Allow the Lord to guide your thoughts and heart during this moment together.

Parting Thoughts

"Since love grows within you, so beauty grows. For love is the beauty of the soul."

SAINT AUGUSTINE OF HIPPO, *CONFESSIONS*

Embarking on a journey of the interior life paves the way for profound transformation that touches every aspect of our being. It is an ongoing pilgrimage that draws us closer to the heart of God as he leads us to revelation, healing, restoration, and spiritual growth.

On a spiritual journey, just as with any journey, you will experience bumps and obstacles in the road, distractions, detours, the mundane, uphill climbs, mountaintop inspirations, and the exhilaration of a downhill trek. Although time alone with the Lord in prayer and contemplation is vital to the spiritual life, equally important is a Christian community, be it family, a small faith-sharing group, a few close spiritual friends, a confessor, or a spiritual director. Community offers encouragement, understanding, and a space to discuss your spiritual experiences and struggles. The transformative nature of the interior life can yield beautiful fruit when shared with a community.

The spiritual journey will bring forth many joys, celebrations, and ah-ha moments, as well as opportunities for healing, forgiveness, and letting go. Spiritual growth, especially healing, is an ongoing process with which you may occasionally require additional help. Reaching a roadblock in your spiritual walk (I am not referring to spiritual dryness or dark nights) may indicate that you need some assistance to get through the impasse. This could be an opportune time to pray and discern whether an advisor, such as a licensed therapist (preferably Christian), inner healing prayer ministry, pastor, spiritual mentor, or healing retreat, may be the next step to get through this season.

As our desert walk with Jesus moves beyond the Lenten season, the ongoing trek takes us deeper into the inner sanctum of our hearts, where we commune in love and friendship with our Lord. Each day is a gift and an opportunity to meet with the resurrected Lord in the intimate and sacred space of our hearts, to seek his face, and to allow him to guide us in love. As Thomas Merton wrote, "And the deepest level of communication is not communication, but communion. It is wordless. It is beyond words, and it is beyond speech, and it is beyond concept."

The graces we receive from our heavenly Father sanctify us as we walk toward our final destination: an integrated, whole, and pure heart full of love. This process will take more than a lifetime to transpire; however, as we journey toward our heavenly home, our hearts can be transformed from the once-arid and desolate desert to a newly cultivated garden full of joy, hope, and the new life that follows the desert rains.

Closing Prayer

"To suffer and to be happy although suffering, to have one's feet on the earth—to walk on the dirty and rough paths of this earth—and yet to be enthroned with Christ at the Father's right hand, to laugh and cry with the children of this world and ceaselessly sing the praises of God with the choirs of angels: this is the life of the Christian until the morning of eternity breaks forth."

SAINT TERESA BENEDICTA OF THE CROSS (EDITH STEIN), *THE HIDDEN LIFE*

Lord, as we move forward in our spiritual walk, may we follow the examples of your beloved who walked hand in hand with you.
May we seek holiness and a heart like Our Blessed Mother.
May we listen to your heartbeat like St. John, your beloved disciple.
May we be spiritually impulsive like St. Peter, responding "yes!" to your call.
May we be astonished like Mary Magdalene every time we encounter you.
May we thirst for you like the Samaritan woman at the well.
May our hearts burn for you like the disciples on the road to Emmaus.
May we always give you thanks like St. Timothy for being counted worthy of serving.
May we be faithful like St. Paul, enduring all hardships for the gospel.
And may we always seek to abide in your presence.

Heavenly Father, we praise you for your love, your goodness, and your mercy. We thank you for the privilege of being called your daughters and sons. We thank you for the gift of your Son, Jesus Christ the Savior, our deliverer, our redeemer, and our friend. Thank you for the Holy Spirit, our advocate, our guide, and our teacher, who leads us into the inner sanctum of our hearts, where we can commune and unite our hearts with yours. Lead us outward, into uncharted waters, to make your name known to the nations. Amen.

Additional Resources

Books

Abide: A Pathway to Transformative Healing and Intimacy with Jesus, Heather Khym (Ave Maria Press, 2022).

Be Healed: A Guide to Encountering the Powerful Love of Jesus in Your Life, Bob Schuchts (Ave Maria Press, 2014).

Boundaries: When to Say Yes, How to Say No to Take Control of Your Life, Henry Cloud and John Townsend (Zondervan, 1992).

Loved as I Am: An Invitation to Conversion, Healing, and Freedom Through Jesus, Sr. Miriam Heidland, SOLT (Ave Maria Press, 2014).

Healing: Bringing the Gift of God's Mercy to the World, Mary Healy (Our Sunday Visitor, 2015).

Mansions of the Heart: Exploring the Seven Stages of Spiritual Growth, R. Thomas Ashbrook (Jossey-Bass, 2009).

Unbound: A Practical Guide to Deliverance, Neal Lozano (Baker Publishing Group, 2010).

Podcasts

Abiding Together with Sister Miriam Heidland, SOLT, Michelle Benzinger, and Heather Khym

Open Doors: Conversations with Heart of the Father with Heart of the Father Ministries

Restore the Glory with Dr. Bob Schuchts and Jake Khym

Healing Retreats/Courses

John Paul II Healing Center (jpiihealingcenter.org)

Christian Healing Ministries (christianhealingmin.org)

Heart of the Father (heartofthefather.com)

Acknowledgments

Where do I begin with thank-yous? At the beginning, of course—a very good place to start.

Mom, you have been and continue to be my biggest cheerleader. No matter what endeavor I undertook—softball, tennis, horse shows, writing—you have always cheered me on and continue to do so. None of your support went unnoticed, and I am eternally grateful. I know I would not have crossed as many finish lines without your encouragement. Thanks, Mom (aka Momzy)!

Dad, you instilled in me a love of learning and reading. You have read enough books in your lifetime to fill our local public library! The subjects you have covered and the places you have visited put you in the running for "the most interesting man in the world." Thank you for reading multiple revisions of *The Desert Walk*. You played an integral role in shaping this book with your invaluable insights. Cheers to learning and reading!

To my everything-person, my husband, Nicolas—*thank you* is not sufficient, but I don't know of any other words in the English language that would express my heart's immeasurable gratitude for you and all you have done in my life. So, thank you for decades of unconditional love, commitment, companionship, friendship, and support. You have shown me how to be a better person; a softer, kinder, gentler version of the person you married decades ago. I could not have finished this book without your inspiration, your encouragement, and the hard conversations about my own need for healing during the writing of *The Desert Walk*. You saw what I couldn't. I am so grateful for the countless revisions that you read. What would I do without you? I love you more and more with each passing day!

Kiddos, you are all grown up now. It's funny how that happens. Now the tides have turned, and all your encouragement and support as I trudged and tumbled through this writing journey helped me finish this project. You are the inspiration behind much of my writing, and I am forever indebted. Thank you for being the greatest kids a mom could ask for and, now, the greatest friends a mom could have.

The "Core Four" is a catchy little name we coined to refer to four friends who came together, connected by our love for the Lord, and began a journey of friendship and sisterhood. I could write a book on the ways we have walked together in the good, the bad, and the messy. Hey, maybe I will write a book! Thank you, Jill, Michelle, and Sasha for being a soft place to land, shoulders to cry on, confidants, healing prayer ministers, and sisters with whom to belly laugh. Your deep faith, wisdom, counsel, and love for our Lord keep me on the straight and narrow, and I wouldn't want it any other way. I thank God for kiddie pools, mutual neighbors, and women's retreats! Core Four, I love you!

Denise, you are my sweet friend, editor, grammar expert, and spiritual challenger with questions that cut to the core. You have read and commented on drafts of *The Desert Walk* for several Lenten seasons. If there's anyone who knows this book inside and out, it's you. Thank you for believing in the book, for not letting me get too distracted with life and my own insecurities, and for reminding me that "this book needs to be published." I will miss our Google Doc comment discussions. Until the next book, dear friend.

To my sisters in Christ, you know who you are. I'm one lucky girl to have you in my life. Whether it's coffee time, walks, dinners, texts, phone calls, ministries, conferences, prayer groups, or floats down a river, I love walking through this life with you, my sisters. You all are the best! Isn't God so good to us?

Thank you to my spiritual director. You get the bird's-eye view, the nitty-gritty, the ups and downs, the sorrows and triumphs, and everything in between. You are faithful and always pointing me to our Lord. I am forever grateful for your spiritual guidance, your poignant questions that reach in and touch my heart, and the countless hours of listening and praying.

And last, but certainly not least, thank you to Liguori Publications. The day I received your email expressing interest in *The Desert Walk* will be forever etched in my memory. Thank you for taking a chance on my story and for believing in its message. I am especially grateful to Fr. Byron Miller for his gentle spirit and evident love for our Lord. I am deeply grateful for his insightful input, wisdom, and kindness throughout my first editing process. His guidance has been invaluable.

Bibliography

"10 Inspirational St. Teresa of Ávila Quotes on Success." Live Online Radio, accessed July 18, 2025, https://liveonlineradio.blog/10-inspirational-st-teresa-of-avila-quotes-on-success.

"An Excerpt from Haruki Murakami's 'Kafka on the Shore.'" LiveJournal, last updated October 7, 2010, https://kulelat.livejournal.com/4654.html.

Angelou, Maya. *On the Pulse of Morning.* New York: Random House, 1993.

Armstrong, Regis J., J.A. Wayne Hellmann, and William J. Short, eds. *Francis of Assisi: Early Documents, Volume 1—The Saint.* Hyde Park, New York: New City Press, 1999.

Attard, Mario, OFM. "Hang It on the Cross." *Catholic Journal*, January 27, 2024. https://catholicjournal.us/2024/01/27/hang-it-on-the-cross.

Augustine of Hippo, *Confessions.* Translated by Henry Chadwick. Oxford, England: Oxford University Press, 1991.

Augustine of Hippo. *Prayers of the Early Church*, edited by J. Manning Potts. London: SCM Press, 1953.

Bethel Music. "Extravagant." *Starlight.* Bethel Music, 2017

Booth, Tom. *Taste of Heaven.* Lake Oswego, Oregon: Oregon Catholic Press, 1999.

Brother Lawrence. *The Practice of the Presence of God.* Translated by John J. Delaney. Image Books, 1977.

Catechism of the Catholic Church, 2nd ed. Washington, DC: United States Catholic Conference, 2000.

Chambers, Oswald. *My Utmost for His Highest*, updated edition, edited by James Reimann. Grand Rapids, Michigan: Discovery House, 1992.

de Chardin, Pierre Teilhard. *Hearts on Fire: Praying with Jesuits*, edited by Michael Harter, SJ. St. Louis, Missouri: St. Louis Institute of Jesuit Sources, 1993.

Chesterton, G.K. *Tremendous Trifles.* New York: Dodd, Mead and Company, 1909.

Dickens, Charles. *The Life and Adventures of Nicholas Nickleby.* London: Chapman and Hall, 1839.

Francis. *Dilexit Nos* (He Loved Us): On the Human and Divine Love of the Heart of Jesus Christ. Encyclical letter, October 24, 2024. Libreria Editrice Vaticana. www.vatican.va/content/francesco/en/encyclicals/documents/20241024-enciclica-dilexit-nos.html.

Gretzinger, Steffany. "Out of Hiding (Father's Song)." *The Undoing.* Bethel Music, 2014.

"The Henry D. Thoreau Mis-Quotation Page." The Walden Woods Project, accessed July 18, 2025, https://walden.org/what-we-do/library/thoreau/mis-quotations.

Henry, Matthew. *Matthew Henry's Commentary on the Whole Bible: Complete and Unabridged in One Volume.* Peabody, Massachusetts: Hendrickson Publishers, 1991.

"Homily of John Paul II." The Holy See, accessed July 18, 2025, https://vatican.va/content/john-paul-ii/en/homilies/1986/documents/hf_jp-ii_hom_19861130_perth-australia.html.

John of the Cross. *The Ascent of Mount Carmel.* Translated and edited by E. Allison Peers. New York: Image Books/Doubleday, 1958.

———. *The Collected Works of St. John of the Cross.* Translated by Kieran Kavanaugh and Otilio Rodriguez. Washington, DC: ICS Publications, 1991.

John Paul II. *You Are the Light of the World.* Combermere, Ontario, Canada: Madonna House Publications, 2000.

Julian of Norwich. *Revelations of Divine Love.* Translated by Elizabeth Spearing, Penguin Classics, 1998.

à Kempis, Thomas. *The Imitation of Christ*, book 3, chapter 27. Translated by William C. Creasy. Notre Dame, Indiana: Ave Maria Press, 2000.

Lewis, C.S. *Letters to Malcolm: Chiefly on Prayer.* New York: Harcourt Brace Jovanovich, 1964.

———. *Mere Christianity.* London: Geoffrey Bles, 1952.

———. The *Problem of Pain.* London: The Centenary Press, 1940.

McCoskey, Pat, OFM. "Saint Francis Novena, Day Four: Humility." *Franciscan Media*, September 28, 2023. https://franciscanmedia.org/franciscan-spirit-blog/saint-francis-novena-day-four-humility.

Merton, Thomas. *The Asian Journal of Thomas Merton*, edited by Naomi Burton, Brother Patrick Hart, and James Laughlin. New York: New Directions Publishing, 1975.

Molla, Gianna Beretta. *The Journey of Our Love: The Letters of Saint Gianna Beretta Molla and Pietro Molla*, edited by Elio Guerriero. New York: Pauline Books & Media, 2011.

Nouwen, Henri J.M. *Out of Solitude: Three Meditations on the Christian Life.* Notre Dame, Indiana: Ave Maria Press, 1974.

———. *The Road to Daybreak: A Spiritual Journey.* New York: Doubleday, 1988.

———. *Sabbatical Journey: The Diary of His Final Year.* Spring Valley, New York: The Crossroad Publishing Company, 1998.

———. *You Are the Beloved: Daily Meditations for Spiritual Living.* New York: Convergent Books, 2017.

Padre Pio. *Letters*. Translated by Geraldine Nolan, Huntington, Indiana: Our Sunday Visitor, 1992.

Penn, William. *No Cross, No Crown*, edited by Anna M. Brinton. Richmond, Indiana: Friends United Press, 2003.

Père Jacques de Jésus. *Listen to the Silence: A Retreat with Père Jacques*. Translated and edited by Francis J. Murphy. Washington, DC: ICS Publications, 2005.

Roach, Becky. "10 Quotes to Help You Meditate on the Exaltation of the Holy Cross." CatholicLink. https://catholic-link.org/10-quotes-to-help-you-meditate-on-the-exaltation-of-the-holy-cross.

Roman Missal, The, 3rd ed. Collegeville, MN: Liturgical Press, 2011.

Rosica, Fr. Michael. "An Extreme Revolution of Holiness: An Insider's Look at Citizenship with the Saints." *Catholic Culture*, January 8, 2008. https://catholicculture.org/culture/library/view.cfm?id=7964.

de Saint-Exupéry, Antoine. *The Little Prince*. Translated by Katherine Woods, New York : Harcourt, Brace & World, 1943.

Stein, Edith. *The Hidden Life: Essays, Meditations, Spiritual Texts*, edited by Dr. L. Gelber and Michael Linssen, OCD. Translated by Waltraut Stein, PhD. Washington, DC: ICS Publications, 2014.

Teresa of Ávila. *The Collected Works of St. Teresa of Ávila: Volume One*. Translated by Kieran Kavanaugh and Otilio Rodriguez. Washington, DC: ICS Publications, 1987.

Thérèse of Lisieux. *Story of a Soul: The Autobiography of St. Thérèse of Lisieux*, 3rd ed. Translated by John Clarke, OCD. Washington, DC: ICS Publications, 1996.

Wintz, Jack, OFM. "St. Anthony: God's Instrument." *Franciscan Media*, June 13, 2023. https://franciscanmedia.org/franciscan-spirit-blog/st-anthony-gods-instrument.

Withers, Bill. "Lean on Me." *Still Bill*. Sussex Records, 1972.

About the Author

Leslie Albizzatti is a Catholic Christian author and ministry leader based in Atlanta. A wife, a mom, and a student of Jesus, she writes from a life shaped by prayer, Scripture, motherhood, and healing ministry to help others encounter God's presence daily.

Leslie has a bachelor's degree from Sweet Briar College and an MBA in international business from the University of Miami. In addition to being a writer, she is a blogger, a speaker, and a board member of the Barnabas Initiative, which seeks to introduce and support evangelistic and discipleship initiatives in the Atlanta area.

Leslie has an ardent heart for women's ministry, inner healing, and prayer groups. She shares weekly faith-based reflections and a monthly devotional newsletter at lesliealbizzatti.com. ***The Desert Walk*** is her first book.